S0-AZV-054 10/16

# Embracing Each Moment

ALSO BY ANAM THUBTEN

*The Magic of Awareness*

*No Self, No Problem*

# Embracing Each Moment

*A GUIDE TO THE AWAKENED LIFE*

Anam Thubten

Shambhala

BOULDER · 2016

Shambhala Publications, Inc.
4720 Walnut Street
Boulder, Colorado 80301
www.shambhala.com

© 2016 by Anam Thubten

All rights reserved. No part of this book may be reproduced in any form
or by any means, electronic or mechanical, including photocopying,
recording, or by any information storage and retrieval system,
without permission in writing from the publisher.

9 8 7 6 5 4 3 2 1

FIRST EDITION
*Printed in the United States of America*

♾ This edition is printed on acid-free paper that meets
the American National Standards Institute Z39.48 Standard.
♻ This book is printed on 30% postconsumer recycled paper.
For more information please visit www.shambhala.com.

Distributed in the United States by Penguin Random House LLC and in
Canada by Random House of Canada Ltd

Designed by Michael Russem

LIBRARY OF CONGRESS CATALOGING-IN-PUBLICATION DATA
Names: Thubten, Anam, author.
Title: Embracing each moment : A guide to the awakened life / Anam Thubten.
Description: First Edition. | Boulder : Shambhala, 2016.
Identifiers: LCCN 2015038923 | ISBN 9781611803464 (pbk. : alk. paper)
Subjects: LCSH: Religious life—Buddhism. | Spiritual life—Buddhism.
Classification: LCC BQ5395 .T486 2016 | DDC 294.3/444—dc23
LC record available at http://lccn.loc.gov/2015038923

# GRATITUDE

So many beautiful souls are gone,
just like the rainbow disappears.
Their faces are smiling in the shrine of my heart.
I've tried to dream them many times,
so I can say "thank you."
These are the most sacred words our lips can utter.
Each time we say them,
this invisible cold ice between us melts.

Thanks to my beloved ones,
You listened to my stories,
Shared thousands of delicious meals,
Opened my heart,
Accepted me the way I am.
Your presence never gave me sorrow,
only joy.
In your field,
my entire being is so relaxed.

Thank you to all my friends.
Your trust empowers me.
Our friendship showed me my own goodness.
The world is less strange because of you.

I'm grateful to the earth for sustaining life,
Cloud for the rain
Flower for its beauty
Sea for its grace
Mountain for its majesty.

Never forget the animals.
Hummingbirds for making me smile by their cuteness,
Squirrels for making me laugh by their mischievousness,
Coyotes for invoking my wildness by their ghostly howling,
This world will be very lonely if they're not here.

I'm even grateful to problems.
They woke me up from my illusions
and led me to the path of compassion.
I would not trade them for anything.

Right now,
Under the full moon's gaze,
I'm writing THANK YOU in the air,
blowing kisses everywhere.
Open your heart
You might get one.

—ANAM THUBTEN

# Contents

# Introduction

THIS HUMAN LIFE IS AN AMAZING MIRACLE. WE CAN FEEL, taste, and touch. We can be sad, fall in love, and feel compassion toward others. Often we are amazed by the cosmic mystery, feeling our unique individuality in the infinite universe and having visions and curiosity about our destiny. We also have a complex cognitive ability that allows us to analyze. Have you ever wondered how you ended up here as a human being? At times we all go through challenges and suffering. In those moments it's not so easy to be a human being. This is a reality that many people experience again and again. We see this in both ourselves and our loved ones. At other times, it's fun to be human. We share delicious food, are enchanted by nature's wonders, and do work that engages and inspires us. In the end, being human is a miracle, and life is a blessing. We all want to be happy. This seems to be our strongest impulse.

From ancient times to the present, people have worked on answering the question of how to achieve happiness. Primarily our happiness comes from our state of mind, though we cannot deny the fact that outside circumstances play a big role. Having our basic needs met can give us physical well-being and lessen our worries about finding food and shelter. Yet more and more we see that genuine happiness comes from deep within. It comes from letting go of our attachments to false beliefs about life and ourselves. It also comes from letting go of old emotional patterns and opening our hearts through love and compassion.

Also we should not be totally focused on ourselves. That makes us small inside and creates a great deal of suffering as well. When we are doing everything exclusively for ourselves, everything that happens to us through the dualistic dance of good and bad is determined in a very rigid way. It may be hard to imagine that we can be free from self-centeredness. Even if we do not completely let go of ego, at least we can be less self-centered. We can open our mind toward the vast state of our own consciousness, boundless love, unconditional joy, fearlessness, and all-encompassing compassion. There is so much we can miss in this world. Being too self-centered not only creates suffering, but it also holds us back from what we can be and experience.

Buddhism has extraordinary teachings that can help us bring more meaning to our everyday life. It helps us grow inside and find true happiness in our various circumstances. Personally, I feel blessed to have found Buddhism. It is the treasure of all treasures. My passion is to share its essential wisdom with others. I do this through teaching, primarily in the West but also periodically in the East. Most Westerners who come to my teachings are interested in the more meditative aspects of Buddhism. They seem to think they can transform their lives once they find the right methods. They're not looking for consolation from a higher power that might be either a divine entity or a supreme human being. This goes along with Buddha's famous statement: "I can show you the way, but your liberation depends on you."

Personally, I feel that I have learned a great deal about the essence of Buddhism by living in the West. The relentless curiosity and inquisitiveness that is the foundation of this modern culture has helped me develop an intimate connection with a living and juicy Buddhism. I'm truly happy to have the chance to teach and practice Buddhism in a world where there is open-mindedness and freedom on so many levels.

This book is based mainly on the public teachings I have offered in the San Francisco Bay Area. Usually the group is a mix of well-seasoned meditators and beginners. Some of them have already practiced Theravada, Vajrayana, or Zen Buddhism, as well as other non-Buddhist traditions. It is nice to be in a group where everyone contributes their own spiritual richness and background. I try, to the best of my ability, to use universal language to explain the core of Buddhist teachings. My intention is to make these teachings clear so that people can practice and integrate them into their everyday lives.

Let me take a moment to express my deepest gratitude to those whose support has made this book possible. There are many volunteers in my community who work hard to make my teachings available to the general public. I thank each of them. They are good-hearted and have the true intention to help others. I feel truly lucky to know these wonderful people. Sharon Roe is one whose constant encouragement is a force that motivated me to put this book together. My ongoing, positive connection with Shambhala Publications is also a blessing. The company's work brings much wisdom to the world. Thank you again. My wish is that this book will help people find clarity and courage, as well as freedom and true happiness, in day-to-day life.

Anam Thubten<br>
Richmond, California

# CHAPTER ONE

# What Buddhism Is All About

THERE ARE TWO KINDS OF LIFESTYLES: SPIRITUAL AND conventional. Some people may think that a spiritual lifestyle involves being a pure vegetarian and not smoking cigarettes or drinking alcohol. But it has nothing to do with what you eat or don't eat. A spiritual lifestyle is all about introspection. When you start practicing introspection, then you are leading a spiritual life.

There are important reflections in which we might like to engage at some point in our lives. Environments such as monasteries and temples encourage us to practice introspection, and there is even a set of traditional reflections that we can follow. These are quite powerful, and millions of people have practiced them. Many practitioners have become awakened. The traditional instructions for introspection can be quite powerful because they are designed to shake up our minds and wake us from the world of illusion and false comfort. Then we can come to realize the importance of this existence. Sometimes in the East, you meet with a spiritual master, like a guru, and even get a set of reflections that is only for you, like a secret teaching.

In Buddhism we ask the question, "What is self?" Many people become awakened from practicing this contemplation. Another reflection we can practice is to ask, "What is the purpose of this human existence?" This is a question we don't ask often in our everyday lives. Actually, it would be strange to raise this question. People might think you were trying to engage them in a philosophical debate. Can you imagine suddenly asking somebody what the purpose of this existence is? Many people have never had a chance to ask such questions. When we don't ask these questions, then we lead unawakened lives.

An unawakened life is not always painful. There is a sense of comfort and psychological solace. It is like having a beautiful dream. I'm sure many of you have had such dreams at some time. Have you ever been having a lovely dream and then something wakes you up? Either your alarm clock goes off, or your dog barks, or a bird starts chirping outside. You wish you could continue your dream. You wish you hadn't been woken up. It could have been a glorious dream. Maybe you were dreaming you were a king—not just a king, but a universal monarch!

We are not happy when someone wakes us up. We all want to continue the nice dream. Now and then, leading an unawakened life is like having a wonderful dream, even though it is based on a total delusion. There is an element of ignorance, as we are unconscious of the underlying reality of this human existence. Of course, leading an awakened life can sometimes be a little bit painful. At the very least, you will have to go through a painful process for a while. It can be painful to lose your psychological solace, your emotional comfort, and your beautiful illusions. Have you ever had such a nice dream that you really did not want to wake up? Did you ever wish that you could live in that dream eternally? Leading an unawakened life can sometimes be quite comfortable. We believe that we have total security and our lives are under control. We know where we are, and we know where we are going.

One reflection that you might like to practice is to keep asking yourself, "What is the purpose of this human life?" This question is very powerful. It has woken up many people throughout history and is taught by all of the Buddhist masters. It is like the sound of the conch in the monasteries during the monsoon retreat. It wakes everybody up. For some people, the question brings a bit of unease and pain too. The pain comes from realizing that our old notions of security and comfort, the ones we are holding on to, are simply illusions. They are like beautiful dreams. We may even feel a bit of existential anxiety for a while, but why are we having this anxiety? We have plenty of money in the bank, and we have the perfect relationship. We are healthy and, not only that, we know everything. What is the matter with us? Feeling this existential anxiety is not always bad. Sometimes it can be quite spiritual. Buddha felt this same anxiety when he was living in the palace surrounded by luxury and ease. He felt it because he started waking up from the illusion of solace and security. Existential anxiety can signal the emergence of spiritual awakening.

When you keep practicing this reflection, you will certainly get many answers. Some of them are going to be quite philosophical.

Someday you may end up thinking the purpose of your life is to become enlightened, which is a very good answer. Most people don't ask this question. They feel that the purpose of this human existence is to survive—not just to survive, but to survive well. This seems to be the purpose of life for most people. We have many different doctrines, ideologies, and formulas describing what is supposed to make us happy. What makes me happy may not make you happy. Some people become happy when they can shave their head and live in the forest. Some become happy when they are able to amass and accumulate an abundance of worldly possessions. Some like to throw a lot of parties or own many homes; then they are very happy. Some people are very happy when they are able to play music, and others are very happy when they are allowed to write poems. Some are happy when they are able to keep themselves busy.

Along with those desires—the desire to survive and survive well—comes anxiety and particularly fear: fear of getting sick, fear of not being able to survive well, fear of being rejected, fear of getting old, fear of dying alone, and fear of not having enough money. So there is a fear in each of us, which is expressed in different colors and forms. Most of the time we are not aware of this fear. It's silent. It's lurking somewhere in our psyche. Perhaps all we need to do is ride a roller coaster for our fear to arise. But sometimes we are ruled by all kinds of fear. This is very much the cause of our suffering. It is the ultimate obstacle.

There are different forms of obstacles: outer, inner, and secret. Some cultures talk about this idea of obstacles more than other cultures. My Tibetan culture constantly talks about obstacles. Usually we ask somebody to pray for us in order to remove obstacles. We go to a temple and do all kinds of beautiful ceremonies to remove obstacles. I haven't heard too much about this idea of obstacles in the West.

We can all understand quite easily what outer obstacles are. They happen in everyday life. Sometimes we have major outer obstacles like getting sick. Then we have minor obstacles happening all the time, like having a flat tire on the highway. That's a form of obstacle. Or maybe the lights go off while you are having a lovely dinner with a bunch of friends so you can't continue the party. That's another form of obstacle. Maybe you lost your car key. That's a minor obstacle.

Then there are inner obstacles, which are psychological. The major inner obstacle is fear. It is an obstacle because it prevents us from becoming infinite. It prevents us from growing inwardly. It prevents us from developing love and compassion. It prevents us from becoming happier. This is why fear is an inner obstacle. The truth is that everyone has his or her own inner obstacles, such as doubt, hatred, anger, and fear. Fear seems to be a universal obstacle.

I'm always talking about the idea of melting. I talk about it per-haps more than anything else these days. I used to talk about enlight-enment quite a lot. Then as time went by, I changed my vocabulary. These days I hardly ever talk about enlightenment. Luckily nobody has complained. Nobody has approached me and said that I don't talk enough about enlightenment. Melting is the experience of not having any sense of being contracted or shut down in any way. Instead, it is having the feeling that you can trust this world, you can trust this universe, and you can trust this human life. It is totally irrational. Just like love; love is irrational. Just like compassion; it is totally irrational. Can you understand the feeling of trusting life? So there is no longer a "you" who is somehow defending your own existence, your own physical territory, your own mental territory, your own egoistic territory, and who is trying to fight or flee from the outer world. This sense of trust comes naturally when you are no longer bound by your own fear. You cannot experience this trust as long as you are ruled by fear. This trust that I am speaking of is also a form of love. It's not so much that you love somebody or something, but that you become love. Usually when we feel love, love toward our dog or toward our friend, we feel a melting happening inside of us. Here you may feel that you become love without any particular object.

Sooner or later you might like to invite your own fears. Maybe you are already conscious of your fears. Invite all of them. Don't suppress them. There are many forms of fear of which you are conscious and many of which you are not aware; there may be a hidden feeling that has been ruling your life all along. A hidden feeling that has been an inner obstacle, holding you back from growing inside, stopping you from becoming more loving and happier. Recognize all of these fears. This is all you need to do. Recognize your own fear. Perhaps you are able to name many of them, but there will also be a list of those you don't know how to name. Perhaps you'll be able to name a whole list of your own fears. Some of these fears are actually funny when you verbalize them. Some of them can be quite dreadful as well, like fear of death. You feel fears in your body too. You may not even be able to identify them.

Recently I was talking with a longtime friend. He and I were trying to summarize all the Buddhist teachings as well as the path. It turned out that it is all about becoming aware of your own limits and learning how to love. Quite simply, this is what Buddhism is all about. Memorize it and perhaps you won't have to buy many more Buddhist books. Let me repeat this. It is all about becoming aware of your own limits and then learning how to love. To become aware of your own limits is to become aware of your own fear. You don't have to reject your fear or transcend it. All you need to do is recognize your fear and be a witness to it.

When you are able to witness your fear, then you feel that there is this ground inside of you, this unshakable ground where you can reside. It can sometimes be physical, or it can be a state of mind or a state of consciousness. The Tantric masters call it the Primordial Fortress. This is the state of conscious in which you cannot be ruled by your own fear. Once you witness your fear, it has no power over you. It begins to lose its grip on you. Soon fear becomes your neighbor. You can dance with it. Eventually fear turns into an ally and becomes your friend and a part of you. Your neuroses become your intelligence. When fear rules you, it becomes a neurosis. When it loses power over you, it becomes intelligence. It helps you survive. It helps you find a way in this life. It helps you get around.

Fear can be a form of intelligence. Without fear, we could never survive. We might walk over a cliff, drink poison, or jump into a fire. So fear is a form of intelligence, not something to be eradicated. Finally you will know how to love because you are no longer ruled by your fear; you can start melting. You don't have to look for happiness. You don't have to search for anything. The secret of happiness is that you can never search for it. If you find something by searching for it, it is not true happiness. It's only psychological solace. You can pursue psychological solace but not true happiness. True happiness comes from loving, melting, and being free from the grip of fear.

# CHAPTER TWO

# Radical Inquiry

THE WORLD IS EMBRACING SCIENCE AS ALMOST THE ULTI-
mate authority on many aspects of reality. People even hope that
science eventually will solve the unknown mysteries, which used to
be solely the domain of spirituality. There has been a movement
in the last few decades to integrate science and spirituality. In the
beginning I had a very strong resistance to that idea. I thought such
integration was going to water down spirituality. I thought integrat-
ing Buddhism and science was going to water down the depth of the
Buddhist teachings. That was my stance. Eventually I changed my
mind, and now I feel strongly about supporting this new movement
and think maybe it's the only way to go. Maybe this integration
of science and spirituality is going to solve many of the problems
we are facing. Maybe it is going to provide a foundation of truth,
intelligence, ethics, and compassion for spirituality.

Amazingly many things of which Buddha spoke thousands of
years ago turned out to be very scientific. A while ago somebody told

me that science is validating the old Buddhist notion of *anatta* (no self). This turned out to be good news—especially for me, because no self has been my trademark. I have been teaching on this subject for many years. I even wrote a book about it. So I am really happy to discover that scientists now are proving the truth of no self.

Many years ago I went to lead a weekend meditation retreat somewhere in Texas. After the retreat, someone gave me a ride to the airport, and before we said farewell, he said, "I have some advice for you. Never again tell Americans that there is no self." This turned out to be devastating news to me because I don't know what else to teach. It is like telling a doctor not to do anything with medicine or telling a stonemason not to touch stone anymore. No self is the truth that Buddha discovered, not based on his bias, but through a long journey of inquiry and deep reflection into the true nature of everything.

Of course, no self is more than "no self." We should not try to understand it literally. When we look around, there is so much evidence that there is indeed a self. So the notion of *anatta* (no self) is not so much about directly rejecting or negating the existence of self. It is pointing out that there is no autonomous, individual self. I know this sounds very philosophical. You may find that this idea is not very useful or relevant to your everyday life. You may find that it will not help you overcome your emotional difficulties. You may find that it will not help you develop love or find unconditional happiness. However the truth is that this wisdom, this truth, is the source from which you will find everything you are longing for.

In Tibetan Buddhist tradition, we often make a subtle distinction between what we call *go ba* and *rtogs pa*, which means intellectual understanding versus direct realization or direct experience. We say that intellectual understanding is a wonderful thing to have, but it has a limitation. Intellectual understanding does not have the potency to bring about a transformation in your consciousness, whereas direct realization has that power, the power to change your consciousness. In this respect we are speaking about the direct realization of *anatta* (no self). You can, of course, read lots of sutras, or books. You can even listen to recordings of teachings like this, and you may end up having quite an impressive and accurate intellectual understanding of no self. You can even get a PhD on it, and still you may find that your intellectual understanding is not transforming your consciousness.

I grew up in Tibet and studied not only the Buddha's teachings but also astrology and poetry. I loved traditional Tibetan poetry, which originated in India. When I was studying poetry, we had to write lots of poems and also read a lot of things about the ocean. The ocean was the most popular metaphor in Indian Buddhist poems. So I wrote many hymns to the ocean without seeing it, because there is no ocean in Tibet. I even developed this affinity with the ocean, hoping that one day I would have a chance to see it. After many years, I finally had the opportunity not only to see the ocean but also to walk on the beach. The first beach I walked on in my life is near San Francisco. The morning I heard that I was going to walk on the beach, my heart was thrilled, filled with all this excitement because I am a devotee of the ocean and wrote many hymns to it. Yet when I got there, I was frightened. I was very afraid of the ocean. I was waiting for the moment when I could leave. This is because the knowledge I had was only an intellectual understanding of the ocean.

Scientifically the wisdom of no self makes total sense. It's about not having any autonomous, independent self inside you. If you look inside and try to find one entity, one speck of a thing that you might like to call a self, in the end you will not find anything. You can search for this individual self all the way from the top of your head to the bottoms of your feet, and you'll end up finding nothing. You can look for it in your body or in your mind, your consciousness, outside yourself or inside yourself. You'll still come up empty-handed. You will not find even one thing that you can call a self. You won't be able to say, "This is who I am. This is my individual self." You'll find that your heart is not your individual self; and your intestines are not your individual self. Your lungs, your head, and your eyeballs are not your individual self. Your consciousness is not your individual self. And sooner or later you will find that even your spirit is not your individual self. A lot of shamanic cultures believe in this spirit, everybody in my family believes in this spirit, and I am hearing that many people in the West believe that there is a spirit. Maybe there is a spirit, but the spirit is not your individual self. Your spirit is not your individual self in the same way that your consciousness and your body are not your individual self. Your soul is not your individual self either.

Recently somebody who is Buddhist asked me how they could find their soul mate. I told them there is no soul mate for a Buddhist. I told them they may have to become a Christian to find a soul mate. There is no soul in Buddhism. Buddha denounced and negated the existence of soul. Maybe there is a soul, but even if there is, that is not your individual self. So you are, or I am, this amazing conglomerate of thoughts, emotions, spirit, awareness, this sacred body, flesh, bones, blood, habits—mental habits as well as karmic habits.

There is a traditional inquiry in my lineage where a master gives you an assignment. Sometimes you have to practice this assignment, a form of inquiry, for a week or even months. The inquiry is to go through every part of your body and search for a personal self. Quite a radical inquiry! There are stories that a master will ask you to go around and shout your names, then the master will meet with you, and he or she will ask you, "Tell me, what did you discover?" If you tell him or her that you discovered your self, then the master will send you back, and you may have to spend another week or month doing the same thing all over again. But if your answer is, "I cannot find myself," that is the true answer.

As I said earlier, now scientists are saying that there is no individual self, and I am very happy about it. So theoretically, scientifically, this notion of *anatta* is making sense, but it is still just another idea, a rational idea. The question is how can we bring this idea alive as a living awareness, a living insight, a breathing insight, so we can experience true transformation. I will ask you to pause and try to imagine your self in this very moment. Can you notice that somebody that is supposed to be who you are is already appearing in your consciousness? That person popping into your head right now is not really who you are. It is a mental image of you. Perhaps you have all kinds of perceptions of that mental image of yourself, of it being wonderful, good, beautiful, not beautiful, intelligent, loveable, bad, and so forth. Can you recognize right now that this is a mental image of you? We have believed in this mental image of ourselves, and we have never questioned the truth that this mental image is who we really are. Sometimes this mental image gets twisted to the extent that we develop unwholesome and negative perceptions about who we are. That is where those serious psychological pathologies sometimes come into being, things like self-loathing and self-hatred.

I have met with many people all over the world who secretly harbor self-loathing and suffering. So much human suffering comes from holding on to the wrong notion of who we are. If you are suffering, I will tell you right now that 95 percent of your suffering is coming from the fact that you are grasping at the wrong notion of yourself. There is no doubt that there is actual suffering in our lives. We hold mistaken notions of ourselves, which not only causes pain and misery but becomes a stumbling block on our journey, the path to awakening to our true nature, which is indescribable and unnameable. Remember, you are nameless in the end. So I am telling you that every notion of yourself is completely wrong. I am telling you directly that all of your ideas of yourself are totally mistaken. I don't have to point out anything to you. I don't have to point out your true nature or your original face. If you want to find someone to point out your original face, I recommend that you find a Zen guy. That's their job. Zen Buddhists are very much into pointing out your original face, your Buddha nature.

Today I cannot point out anything to you or to myself. The only thing I can do is reveal an illusion inside you, a falsehood inside you. I am revealing the falsehood, the illusory nature of your idea, your notion of who you are. This is all I need to do. So here I am searching and witnessing this lie, this illusion, this falsehood in your consciousness. I am asking you to wake up and realize it so you can let go of your grasping, let go of your identification with all these false notions of yourself. When you are able to do that, you are also going to experience this amazing freedom where much of your guilt will go away, much of your shame will disappear suddenly, and all these miseries will leave you once and for all.

Now you know the essence of every teaching that Buddha gave. Now you know the essence of every sermon that Buddha offered. This is the most amazing truth that you can hear in this lifetime, the truth of no self. Try to love this truth. Try to direct your attention into it. You might also like to dedicate time, energy, zeal, and effort into realizing this liberating truth. In the East, we find many people meditating. Some people have meditated for ten years or even longer than that. What they are trying to do is go through this shift from intellectual understanding to direct experience. For some people, it takes many years to have that shift. For some people, it does not take any time at all.

There is a difference between being a spiritual seeker and just being spiritual. You can be spiritual and also be very conventional. There are lots of conventional spiritual people and conventional Buddhists. There are around four or five hundred million conventional Buddhists. Do you know what they do? They go to Buddhist conventions. Hundreds and thousands of people get together, and everybody is Buddhist. Usually they pick up myths, romantic myths, when they go to these conventions. They talk about the same thing, and they worship the same object. So you can be a conventional Buddhist, and you can be a conventional spiritual being too. But if you want to be a true seeker, a true spiritual seeker, then you have to invite this radical inquiry into your life. The inquiry, which is truly radical, asks who you are in the ultimate sense. Once you have invited this radical inquiry, sooner or later you are going to realize the falsehood of your perception of yourself. Along with that, you are going to lose much of your misery, which is not bad news. You will lose most of your suffering. You will lose most of your sorrow, most of your guilt, and most of your shame.

There is another way to let go of this falsehood, and that is to offer it. You can offer it right now. And you won't have much choice except to really spend some time and effort in discovering this truth. I'll tell you why you don't have too many choices. First, I am begging you to discover this truth. Next, scientists are also telling you that this is true. So do you have any choice now? Not too much. Once the scientists get onboard, you really won't have much choice. The scientists told us that the world is round, and of course, many people tried to resist that idea, trying to prove that the world is flat. But today you see that people wound up believing the world is round. Just like that. Sooner or later you have no choice except to let go of this illusion of the individual self. If you don't believe me, next time I may invite a group of scientists. We may together demonstrate the falsehood of your individual self. Then you won't have any more choice. The highest level of joy and happiness comes from letting go of grasping at the illusion of individual self.

# CHAPTER THREE

# Hymns to Ordinary Things

THERE ARE MANY FORMS OF SUFFERING IN THIS WORLD. Some of them are quite palpable when they take the form of crises. Other times suffering can be quite subtle. It can be a phenomenon that runs through our everyday lives. Buddha was very aware of this human situation, the fact that suffering is always part of this human life. He also realized that most of the time people are not even conscious that they are suffering. So in the beginning, he invited all of his disciples to meditate not on the absolute, the divine, but on human suffering, collective as well as individual. That turned out to be revolutionary in Buddha's time, because until then spiritual practice was all about merging yourself with all of these holy and divine dimensions, like the Supreme Truth. Buddha felt that we cannot grow inside nor can we be at true peace unless we invite this courageous awareness, which is to be aware of both collective and personal suffering. His path is not to escape to caves in the Himalayas and become a glutton who indulges in pseudospirituality that provides a false solace. Instead, his path is to engage with this world and witness the pervasiveness of human misery—sickness, injustice, poverty, and mental crises. Buddha also asked everybody to go inside, meditate on their own personal suffering, and find out its root cause.

The idea of spiritual awakening is prevalent in many of the great traditions of the East. Even today, you've probably noticed that there is a collective longing for spiritual awakening, even though sometimes we don't have a clear idea of what that is. This idea of spiritual awakening used to be called enlightenment. Of course, you can play with this idea of spiritual awakening. It sounds very good, but at the same time, part of the inevitable process of this inner awakening is to completely shake the ground of your conditioned mind. You cannot wake up unless you have this willingness to shake up your mind. Just like sometimes when you are in bed, someone has to shake you in order for you to wake up. The mind has to be shaken from its deep confinement of conditioning and all its habits. When the mind wakes up, then it becomes aware of everything. It becomes naturally aware of your pain. It becomes aware of many things about you. It also becomes aware of the fact that you are suffering. It becomes aware of the fact that you have been taking refuge in false sanctuaries for a very long time. It becomes aware of the fact that you have been living in a beautiful bubble that is going to burst at any given moment. Pretty much you can say that all forms of security are just another form of those illusory, beautiful bubbles. Anything that you take refuge in as a source of comfort or glory or to prove that you have control over your life is just a beautiful bubble. And you may realize that even your existence is another bubble. Your existence is truly beautiful, but at the same time, it is very fragile. It can fall apart at any given moment.

There is a verse that we chanted in the monasteries of Tibet during the yearly summer retreat. It is a verse that was supposed to have been spoken by Buddha. This verse invites you to reflect deeply on your life. Not from the point of view of your conditioned mind, but from a courageous and intelligent awareness. This verse says that we must regard our existence as dew. Think of a dewdrop on a blade of grass. You know how exquisite it is. If you are a skilled photographer, you can zoom your camera in on that tiny dewdrop on the grass in the early morning. It can be a truly beautiful picture. You capture its eternal beauty one moment, and in the next moment it may be gone. Just like that our existence is truly exquisite and fragile at the same time.

So when the mind is shaken from its confinement of comfort and all of its habits, it becomes aware of everything. We become aware of the fragile reality of our own existence. We also become aware of what is happening in our bodies as well as in our hearts and minds. We may begin to feel the pain that we have been suppressing in our hearts. Or we may become aware of a contraction somewhere in our bodies to which we have previously been oblivious. Or we may become aware of a veil or blindness somewhere in our consciousness that we were unfamiliar with before.

There are many forms of suffering, but one of the universal forms of suffering that many people are dealing with is this deep sense of emptiness inside themselves. We all have that. There is a lack inside each of us. When we allow ourselves to feel it completely, it becomes very painful. So we try to shut down such awareness with every means at our disposal. We use chocolate, candy, coffee, and wine to shut down that awareness completely. There are so many means available to us. We can indulge in all forms of entertainment. We can watch movies. We can go to parties. We can have an unending internal monologue. It's a form of mental gossiping. No delicious food, no parties, but at least we can entertain our minds with mental gossiping; chatting and talking to our own minds and keeping ourselves completely distracted. There are lots of beautiful illusions that we can create in this life, beautiful bubbles like the idea of achievement and the idea of security. Perhaps we can amass a fortune and tell ourselves that somehow we are succeeding in life and fulfilling all our dreams. They're all just beautiful illusions, which have no concreteness in themselves. They are like castles in the sky that are ready to collapse at any given moment. But somehow we feel the symptoms of this inner emptiness, and this is why we are always looking for something. We are looking for friendship, looking for love, looking for achievement. We are always looking for something. Our hearts are filled with this insatiable desire all the time.

Recently I heard that many people in this country feel that there is an emptiness within them. They feel that they don't have enough friends in their lives, which is somehow totally paradoxical because they have social media and can connect with thousands of people in a single instant, which is quite amazing. At the same time, many people are feeling that they don't have enough friends. So people are looking for true friends. People are looking for love. People are looking for more and more possessions, material possessions. Some people make an unbelievable fortune and still feel an insatiable desire. They feel that they need more. So most of the time, a lot of the suffering we face in this modern time is coming from this inner emptiness. The pain of this inner emptiness can be so overwhelming that sometimes it can force people to become addicts. They become addicted to substances they use to numb this pain. People use all kinds of things to numb the pain. They can be workaholics or be addicted to shopping.

The initial state of inner awakening is to go inside and feel everything that is hidden inside your heart, including the pain, the loneliness, the pain of the inner emptiness of wealth. Soon you will realize that this inner emptiness is coming from not being able to realize the beautiful truth that pervades everything, pervades this entire universe. This truth is the all-pervasive sacredness. We are missing the sacredness. One of the greatest tragedies of the twenty-first century is that we are losing our connection to this truth of sacredness. Of course, there are many good things that we can praise about this twenty-first century. Many wonderful developments have happened in this modern time. There are many unbelievable technological innovations and medicines that cure disease. So there are many things that we can praise about the achievements of our modern age. But there is a spiritual crisis happening, and that is losing our connection with this truth, the truth of the all-pervasive sacredness of everything.

Sacredness is not a belief system. It is a timeless truth. It is always there, just like the clouds in the sky. Just like the trees growing in the mountains, sacredness is always there. It is part of this existence. The consequence of losing our connection with this truth can sometimes be quite dangerous. And when we lose this understanding, we develop a very mechanical relationship with the world, within as well as without. We develop a very mechanical relationship with ourselves and also with the outer world, the world of nature, and with humanity as a whole. When we lose our understanding, we develop mechanical relationships with humanity, and we don't know how to feel love toward others. Then people objectify each other.

Actually, objectifying people is a big habit in this world. Women have been objectified. Men have been objectified too. Throughout history, women have been objectified because people have lost this understanding of sacredness and are having mechanical relationships. This is why the Tantric Buddhists have come up with fourteen *samayas* (sacred commitments). The last one, the fourteenth, is not morally disparaging to women, does not regard women as inferior. This means not objectifying them, and it includes men as well. The commitment is to not objectify men or women, not to objectify people, but to feel this sacredness in all relationships so you can feel reverence, love, and genuine kindness toward others.

When we have a mechanical relationship with the world of nature, we see the world as just objects without spirits, so we just want to use them for our own desires. This is what we have been doing throughout our history. We have been abusing the world of nature, and now we see the devastating consequences of conquering that world.

[ 26 ]

Also we have lost, for a long time actually, the sacredness in our relationship with the world of living entities. For many cultures, including the Tibetan culture, everything is sacred. In particular, the Tibetan shamans believe that everything is alive; everything is an expression of spirit, whatever that is. They feel that trees are alive. They feel that rocks, stones, and rivers are alive. They also feel this sacredness in their relationships with living entities, meaning animals. In many indigenous cultures, before they kill an animal, hunters ask permission to take its life. They totally revere the animal as an expression of that universal spirit. So they feel that sacredness in their relationship to everything, with the world of nature and with the world of living beings.

I read somewhere that a renowned Tibetan master came to the West in the sixties to teach, and they asked him what he was going to teach. He said he would teach people how to feel the sacredness of everything. But remember, sacredness is not a belief system. So it is not entirely a religious matter. It's not even a Buddhist thing. It's not a Buddhist belief system or Hindu belief system. Can you say that a rainbow is a Buddhist belief system? We walk on the beach sometimes, and we feel there is beauty everywhere. Can you say that beauty is a Buddhist belief system or not? This goes beyond Buddhism, and it has nothing to do with Buddhism in the ultimate sense. The question is how we can feel that we are tuning in to this truth that seems to be invisible and yet is all-pervasive, so we may be able to feel this sacredness in relationship to ourselves and in relationship to people and the world of nature as well as all living beings.

The question is, how can we feel this sacredness? One of the main purposes of the ceremonies and rituals that exist in the wisdom traditions is to shake up our minds and feel this sacredness. There are many forms of rituals. There are Zen Buddhist rituals and Tibetan Buddhist rituals. On the surface, they are quite different from each other. The Zen Buddhist rituals are very subtle, while Tibetan Buddhist rituals are very colorful. Of course, we can turn rituals into compulsions when we do them without any awareness. But when we do them with awareness, they can sometimes be a powerful catalyst to shake up our minds and feel the sacredness. This is why many people cannot feel the sacredness in the ordinary world. They have to go to a temple so they can feel it.

Even ordinary silence can be a ceremony, a ceremony that allows us to pause and step out of our conditioned minds. This may allow us to feel the all-pervasive sacredness. The truth is we don't have to go to a monastery to learn how to do a ceremony or rituals. Life is full of rituals and ceremonies. You can turn everything into a ritual. You can turn cutting the grass into a ceremony, a sacred ritual. You can turn drinking tea into a ritual. You may light candles as a ritual. You can turn walking in the woods into a ceremony. This is why Tibetan cultures have many hymns to praise ordinary things in life, such as tea. There is one particular hymn, a praise that is very popular. It is called *cha bstod*. *Cha* means "tea," and *bstod* means "hymns." Usually you have religious hymns, hymns to God or hymns to the divine. But the Tibetans come up with hymns to tea, hymns to the ordinary things. You can write hymns to ordinary things, like the tree growing in front of your house. One day you may be writing hymns to your carpet or your pillow. Of course, that is a sign that you are losing your mind. Now and then you have to lose your mind to wake up. Above all, when you know how to pause, then anything you do in life can be a ritual. So the pause, the art of pausing, is the most essential thing to learn.

This is what Buddha taught, the art of pausing. Buddha said to be aware that you are breathing in while you are breathing in. How simple it is. Buddha also said to be aware of walking while you are walking. The moment you become aware of what you are doing, there is a pause. That pause is you somehow stepping out of the conditioned mind. You are breaking that never-ending, nonstop way of the conditioned mind. The conditioned mind is sometimes called the monkey mind, or the samsaric mind in some traditions. The moment you allow yourself to become completely aware of what you are doing, there is a pause in your consciousness. In that pause, your conditioned mind is no longer operating. There is a "restedness." If you allow yourself to be in that restedness, then you may feel this sacredness everywhere. When you feel this sacredness everywhere, the awareness of this sacredness becomes the true medicine. Only this medicine can heal the disease that is almost epidemic right now. The disease of being empty inside, feeling that you are lacking something, feeling that you are not rich, that you are not complete inside. This is a way that we can feel true fulfillment. This is how we can finally realize unconditional happiness.

There are many theories on how to achieve happiness. As you know, people are constantly developing techniques and theories about how to achieve it. The truth is the only way you can achieve unconditional happiness is by knowing how to tune in to this truth, this subtle and pervasive truth, the sacredness of everything. Then your relationship with people becomes alive and filled with reverence and love, and you no longer objectify people. Finally you know how to feel unconditional love. Then you may feel that this world is your home, even though it sometimes has a lot of imperfections. It is still your home. You may feel that this world is heaven. Not heaven as you thought, but heaven with lots of imperfections. Then you may feel this spirit everywhere in the world of nature, in the trees and animals. You may feel a deep reverence and heart connection with everything that exists. You'll find that you are a modern mystic. You'll be a mystic whose heart is drunk with love. In the end, the emptiness you felt as a terrifying condition and tried to get rid of by all kinds of creative means turned out to be sacred, a doorway to your aloneness that was always perfect and lacked nothing.

# CHAPTER FOUR

# The Buddha of Love

THE BUDDHA MAITREYA IS CONSIDERED THE BUDDHA OF the future. His name, Buddha Maitreya, translates as the "buddha of love." To me, Buddha Maitreya is an archetype, a sacred allegory representing something profound and innate in each of us, our innate love. Love is innate to all of us, and we can regard love and compassion as our basic instincts. Our basic instincts are not all dark and impure. Love is our most basic human instinct, along with intelligence, compassion, and courage. There is love in all of us. There is even universal love, all-embracing love, in all of us. This is part of who we are. There are many forms of love. Love comes in a variety of flavors and textures. We experience love for family members, love for friends, love for animals, and love for the world of nature. Love is this authentic feeling that transcends judgment, hatred, and envy. It embraces one person or a group of people in our hearts with trust and kindness. This unconditional acceptance and affinity is what love is.

We feel love for many people in our lifetime, and it is quite easy to love the world of nature—the beautiful forest, the majestic mountains. Our hearts open when we are standing before sunsets or mountains or great rivers. We all love nature easily. We don't have to meditate for a long time or go through psychoanalysis to love nature. At a very early age, we humans start demonstrating our intrinsic love toward the world of nature as well as toward the animal kingdom. We love animals most of the time. It is easy to love our pets, and of course, they love us unconditionally. They often show their unconditional love and their loyalty toward us. Not only that, they are extremely charming most of the time. Some animals are much easier to love. Those little dogs you see now and then are so sweet and adorable!

However, our love toward humanity is very complicated. When we love a human being, that love can be quite heroic. Perhaps it is much more heroic or profound than our love of nature or anything else. When we really love somebody, we are able to sacrifice ourselves. We have this selfless, big heart, through which we can have the willingness to carry the other person's suffering and pain. And we can have unquestioning determination to share our happiness, our glory, and our richness with that person. It is said that this kind of love toward all living beings was felt by Buddha himself all the time. Many great, awakened masters felt this love too.

At the same time, it is very difficult to love humanity. When you walk on the street or drive on the highway, try to look around. Make sure you look around and recognize all the human beings. Can you love them? Can you find sacredness, holiness, or some kind of charming quality in them? You know that sometimes it is very difficult to open your heart and find the beauty and holiness in human beings that you can find quite easily in nature or even animals. That is why many people have a much easier time loving animals than loving human beings. Sometimes it is very difficult to accept human beings with their complex personalities. Yet this is the only way we can evolve. Sooner or later, we must learn how to love all humanity. We must learn how to recognize the charm, the sweetness, and the adorable qualities in humanity without any exclusions. Perhaps we may think that such love is impossible, but the truth is that this love is very possible. Having this love in your heart is the only way you can evolve. It is the only way you can find healing, transformation, and true happiness. So Buddha Maitreya, the future buddha, is only an archetype. We all are future buddhas. We all are the Buddha Maitreya. The Buddha Maitreya symbolizes this all-embracing love.

One time, the Buddhist master Asanga was meditating in the forest. He was hoping that soon he would see a divine vision of Buddha Maitreya. He meditated for twelve years without any sign of achievement. After meditating for twelve years in the forest and hoping to see the divine vision of Buddha Maitreya, he was quite disappointed. He decided to quit his quest. On the way home, he ran into a wounded dog lying on the street. This poor dog's entire body was covered with maggots. He felt genuine love and compassion toward this wounded dog. He wanted to help it and remove all the maggots eating its body. First he tried to remove the insects with his hands, but then he also felt love and compassion toward those insects. He was afraid of killing them with his hands. He decided to remove them with his tongue. The sight was so grotesque he could not touch the maggots with his tongue while his eyes were open. He closed his eyes and stuck out his tongue. Suddenly there was no more wounded dog. He had a vision of Buddha Maitreya. Of course, this is a very famous story that you don't have to take literally. It can be a metaphorical story. You are Buddha Maitreya, and you are the future buddha. There is an all-embracing love inside you. You are born with it. This is your basic instinct. You just have to find a way to rekindle it.

Again, there are many forms of love. There is spiritual or divine love. This is love without any object, which is a very powerful love. There are many beautiful and powerful practices than can help us to evoke this spiritual, objectless love. Most of the time, our love has an object. True spiritual love, divine love, has no object. This is why the Hindus often practice bhakti yoga, which is the yoga of divine love. You can feel this spiritual love, love toward Avalokiteshvara, love toward Guanyin. Guanyin is not an object. Avalokiteshvara is not an object. The truth is that you will never find Avalokiteshvara from outside. As a Mahayana and Tantric Buddhist, I have practiced many *sadhanas,* Buddhist versions of bhakti yoga. For a long time, I practiced the Avalokiteshvara *sadhana.* I felt this profound, almost transcendent level of love toward Avalokiteshvara. For a long time, I wanted to see Avalokiteshvara. Of course, in the end I could not find Avalokiteshvara because Avalokiteshvara is not an object. When you can't find Avalokiteshvara and still love Avalokiteshvara, that is true spiritual love that is transcendent love. I am not asking you to start doing bhakti yoga or Tantric Buddhist *sadhanas* to try and feel this objectless love. All I am saying is there is a tradition of cultivating and invoking this transcendent and spiritual love. I am not saying that this is the only way to freedom. I am not even telling you that you must do such spiritual practice, or *sadhana*.

The purpose of invoking that transcendent love is to melt all of our fear, to melt all of our hatred and to loosen our attachment, our grasp of ourselves. We can experience this profound feeling of melting through different forms of love, through spiritual love or love of humanity. Of course, sometimes love is misunderstood. When we think we love somebody, sometimes it turns out not to be pure love. It often can be mixed or poisoned with our own selfish motives and projections. This kind of poisonous love is often found in human relationships. I felt love toward my spiritual masters when I was young. It was a very interesting love. It wasn't romantic love. It wasn't tribal love. My love for my relatives and friends was more tribal love. The love I felt toward some of my spiritual masters was unique. It had elements of trust and reverence. In many ways, my love was pure. But as you know, love can sometimes be misused. Love can sometimes be poisoned with our own neuroses. When you think you love somebody, it is not true love. Sometimes we can have true love, but it can be mixed up with our own neuroses. One time a monk fell in love with the Buddha. He always showed up in the presence of the Buddha. He could not take his gaze away from the Buddha. This is a famous anecdote mentioned in some of the earliest Buddhist sutras. One day Buddha kicked him out. The monk was totally lost in despair. With that feeling of rejection and despair, he was awakened. He eventually became enlightened. He had authentic love for the Buddha, but his love was mixed with lots of projections.

Love heals everything. Love will awaken you. It heals your wounded heart and will awaken your deluded consciousness. Love of humanity is, in the end, the only true love. You may have divine love, but if you don't know how to love humanity, your love is incomplete. In the end, the highest love is not spiritual love nor transcendent love. It is not the love of Avalokiteshvara. It is not the love of Guanyin. It is not love of Shiva. The highest love you can find, love that will free you and heal you, is your love of humanity. Once you love humanity, you can love everything. Then you won't say, "Well, I love humanity, but I don't know how to love a rainbow. I don't know how to love a beautiful sunset. I have to go to some kind of spiritual workshop or shamanic ceremony so I can let go of all my frozen love, so I can finally love the beautiful beach." I promise that once you love humanity, there is only love inside you. Loving humanity is the most powerful love, but it is the most difficult to actualize.

Shantideva said, "When you look at others, remember to gaze with a loving eye." What he said sounds so simple, not very profound. At least it is not philosophically profound. We all know what he is saying. He is saying to remember to look at others with a loving expression. He is speaking literally, not metaphorically. It would be transformative for us to memorize this simple message given by Shantideva, the most amazing bodhisattva in human history. Every day you might at least like to remember this message and remember to gaze at somebody with a loving expression. You can do that toward your family members or your neighbor or a stranger. Of course, you have to be a bit careful going outside and looking at somebody with a loving expression. As you know, this modern culture has many hang-ups. People may think you are a little crazy or that you want something from them. You can look at yourself with a loving expression. You can look at everybody with the loving eye of compassion.

There is an eye of consciousness, the eye of the heart. It is not a physical eye. It is the wisdom eye. It is the eye of the dharma. The eye of the heart is compassion. You can gaze, you can look at all humanity, and your visualization is with the eye of compassion. In the same way, from morning all the way to evening, you run into many people, those whom you love or those with whom you have difficult issues, like resentment or judgment. You might like to remember practicing the simple message from Shantideva. Gaze and look at all of them with the eye of compassion, with the eye of love. Sometimes you don't have to express it outwardly, and other times you can express it outwardly. Whenever you feel this all-embracing love toward humanity, finally everyone you connect with will be touched by that love. Your fear will go away. Your suffering will vanish along with your paranoia and jealousy. You will feel that you are in harmony with the universe and with the fleeting circumstances of life. You will feel this unconditional joy in the face of crisis.

The question is, how can we bring about this all-embracing love of humanity? It is not a question of whether or not you know how to love. It's more a question of resistance. There is a resistance in each of us, a resistance to love. There is a resistance to letting go of our fear, our judgment, our own version of duality. This manifests as the resistance to loving all of humanity.

Buddha said the true monk is not someone with a shaved head who goes around begging for food, but someone who has conquered his own doubt. Buddha often talked about doubt being a powerful hindrance on the spiritual path. The doubt that the Buddha was talking about can be interpreted in many ways. It can be understood as doubt toward the dharma, doubt toward enlightenment, or doubt toward the path of love and compassion. Here, I will interpret this doubt as more of a resistance. It is a resistance to love. Resistance is a form of doubt, isn't it? In the same way, doubt is a form of resistance. We might like to go inside ourselves and find out about this doubt. Love is very scary, very frightening to the ego. This fear keeps us from letting go of all our defenses. It keeps us from jumping into that both scary and liberating world of all-embracing love.

Once you go inside and find that resistance, how can you let go of it? You might like to ask yourself this question, "What would happen if I let go of this resistance?" If you listen to the ego, ego will offer false logic and false reasons why you should not let go of your resistance. Your ego will tell you are going to die. It will say you will lose control over your mind and then you won't know how to tell between people you should love and people you should not love, which sounds crazy. But if you have a moment, listen to your deepest wisdom. That wisdom will tell you that when you open your heart, you are going to be free and happy forever. Sometimes you may have to keep this love a secret. You can't tell some people that you love everybody. They may not like to hear that, especially if they feel that you have to love them more than anybody else. Let this love live in your heart. At first, this love will be small, like a candle burning in the wind. Then slowly this love will evolve inside you. It will grow. This love will heal everything. Eventually you will be able to love everything. You will be able to love this entire existence, with its beauty as well as its messiness.

# CHAPTER FIVE

# Surrender to the Unknown

A Tibetan master named Rigdzin Godem said there is only one ground, yet there are two paths. Because of that, there are two fruitions. When he said that there are two paths, he was talking about the path of awareness and the path of unawareness. We have a choice to walk the path of awareness or the path of unawareness. Many people walk the path of unawareness. Of course, we cannot go around and figure out who is walking the path of awareness and who is walking the path of unawareness. So this idea of awareness and unawareness are two different states of mind or consciousness.

There is also collective unawareness because many people are literally abiding in that unawareness. Unawareness can sometimes be quite heavy and painful. Not only that, it can serve as the root of all violence and suffering, including that which we are witnessing in today's world. Of course, violence, aggression, and suffering are not new. They have been on this planet from the very beginning of human civilization, and we must remember that they have been here all that time. Also, we might like to realize that the root of all our individual as well as collective problems is that collective unawareness. Sometimes we are part of the collective unawareness. Not only that, we can even be contributors to it. Collective unawareness is the basis of a host of delusions.

We won't be able to count or go through each of those delusions here, but there are two major delusions we can illuminate. They are the notions of certainty and security. These notions do not exist at all. They are absolutely a big myth, just our mental fabrications. Yet the whole world believes that certainty is a state that we can achieve, maintain, and hold on to. We also believe that having some sort of security is going to make us happy. We are going to somehow fulfill our desires as well as fill this basic emptiness that we all have inside. When we use all of our resources, mental as well as physical, to actualize such illusions, then we become neurotic. We easily become irrational, and then before you know it, we become destructive. We become destructive towards ourselves as well as towards others. We tend to sacrifice our basic sanity, our love, our compassion, and even our dignity in order to achieve these illusions.

The most profound insight we can gain is the realization that there is no certainty and no security in this world. Let me tell you a Tibetan parable. One time there was a beggar who was wandering around begging for food and grain. At one point, he was able to accumulate enough barley that he had this huge sack of it. He was quite happy. It was the best achievement of his life. He felt more relief and more happiness than he had ever felt before. He decided to take a little break. He saw a house and decided to sleep underneath it. He tied the big sack of barley to one of the rafters, and then he lay down to sleep. But he couldn't fall asleep because his heart was racing with so much joy. Then he started planning his future. The first thought that popped into his mind was that he was going to make a business out of that bag of barley. Soon he would be a wealthy man. It was just a matter of time. Soon he would get married and have a child, a son. This thought made him very excited. He started thinking about what he would name his son. He had a bit of a problem coming up with an auspicious name. Just then, the moon was rising, and he decided to call his son The Famous Moon. All this time, a big rat was gnawing on the rope that held the big sack to the rafter. Soon the rope was broken, and the big sack fell on his head and killed him. Nevertheless, this is called the parable of the father of The Famous Moon.

In Tibet, we often tell this parable to remind ourselves that there is no certainty. Even though we know this, we are constantly living in the future. We are always planning, and we have these strong ideas that we are going to do this or that tomorrow. We are going to achieve things sometime down the road. There is nothing wrong with having plans and strategizing about how we are going to create our future. But often we are very attached to our ideas and our dreams, our visions and our hopes regarding the future. Then we want to have certainty that they will be realized. We become frightened, scared, and neurotic when we see the signs popping up here and there indicating that things are uncertain. We can never have certainty regarding the future. We can never have absolute influence, control, or certainty over how our lives and events are unfolding.

Another delusion that we are attached to is this thing called security. There are all kinds of security that we want to have. We want to achieve security through many means. We try to achieve it through relationships—not just romantic relationships, but all forms of relationships. We also try to have security through money, wealth, and also through successful and promising careers. The more we try to hold on to the notion of security, the more neurotic we become. A large portion of the human neuroses that you may be witnessing in yourself or recognizing in others comes from this desire for absolute security. The truth is that there is no security. We may die this evening, or we may not die for a very long time. Most probably we are going to live for a long time. Also, there is no guarantee that our houses are always going to be there. We cannot be 100 percent sure that money in the bank is always going to be there. Everything that we love, that we cherish, that we hold on to, including our health, can go away. It can dissolve right where it is without any warning signs.

Recently I visited Hawaii, and one of my longtime friends, a very courageous lady, had a stroke and couldn't attend the meditation retreat I led. I decided to pay her a visit in the hospital. When I got there, she couldn't talk. She couldn't utter even one word. I looked at her and saw that her courageous spirit was still present. She hadn't lost that. I couldn't ask her how she was doing because she didn't have the ability to say anything. I sat in her presence for a while and sent my love. I offered my prayers that she would be OK. I wished I had some kind of divine power, some kind of secret I could use to heal her right there. But the truth is that no matter how much good-hearted intention I had toward her, in the ultimate sense, there was nothing I could do, though I hoped that my prayers would have an impact on her recovery. I started talking to her, but I didn't tell her she was going to be healed. I didn't say that my prayers and blessings would cause her recovery. I told her, "I offered my prayers, and I wish that you will be healed, but you must be courageous because there is no certainty, no absolute certainty that you are going to be cured." I told her, "This is a moment when you must surrender to the unknown. You must be ready to face all events. You must be ready to face the worst nightmare, the most difficult situation." So far I haven't heard any news from her even though I asked some *sangha* members to keep me informed about her health. There is no certainty right now whether she is ever going to be healed. She may never be able to speak again in this lifetime. It was very challenging for me to tell her that there is no certainty and that she has to be courageous. She may have to face the worst condition. But I also told her that this was going to be an amazing opportunity for her. I told her that she could be completely happy no matter what happens if she is courageous and has the wisdom to surrender to life itself as well as to the great unknown, if she has the courage to let go of all her desires and attachment to certainty and security. I started to see a little bit of a smile on her face just before I left.

The truth is that the only way we can find freedom, the only way we can find true happiness, unconditional happiness, and unconditional joy is actually from becoming aware of and learning to love this basic truth of reality, which is the lack of security and certainty. In the beginning, we may feel a bit of unease, or we may feel shocked.

We may even feel some kind of existential anxiety by awakening to this basic truth of reality. It's not just that we as individuals have no basic, fundamental security or certainty. The whole world, the whole existence, the whole universe also lacks basic certainty and security. Buddha felt this, but then he was awakened to this truth. He felt a bit of discomfit; he felt unease for a while. That is why Buddha said, "This world lacks essence. It trembles in all directions, and I long to find myself in a place unscathed by such conditions, but I cannot see such a place." This verse is found in one of the Pali sutras, which are considered the oldest recorded teachings of the Buddha. So Buddha was expressing that even he felt this unease, almost some kind of existential anxiety, realizing that this world, this life, this universe, this existence, has no essence. It is ready to fall apart at any given moment. It is ready to dissolve. It is fragile, whimsical, and transient. It is also truly beautiful and mysterious, sometimes divine, and sometimes ordinary too. Sometimes we can understand what it is all about, and sometimes we have no idea what it is all about. Once we are awakened to that fundamental truth of all things, which is that they lack security and certainty, we will need some time to make friends with that new reality. Then some day we will love that truth completely, and we will end up loving that truth as we used to love the illusion of security and certainty.

We all know that chasing after illusion only causes pain and suffering. It makes us greedy and selfish. It makes us irrational. It makes us lose all our dignity as well as our integrity. The truth is that most of the time, we don't know we are actually suffering. There is a lot of suffering and pain in trying to secure our illusions. Most of the time, we are not aware of that suffering. Try to imagine that you are having an amazing relationship. You may find lots of comfort in that relationship. As far as you can tell, that relationship is working for you. You think that it is a blessing from some divine source. That relationship may be everything in your mind, but if you inquire, you find that there is fear. There is insecurity. There is fear somewhere in your heart about the prospect of losing that relationship. In the same way, you may have a lot of wealth. When you look carefully, you'll find something else. But if you don't inquire, you may find a lot of joy, comfort, and happiness from having so much wealth in your life because you can do anything you want to do. You can have three houses, you can go on a cruise, you can buy nice cars, you can throw huge parties, and you can hire many people. You can do anything you want to do. But when you look carefully, there is also insecurity that is unseen, unspoken.

We also try to find solutions in the spiritual world. Many years ago, I gave a teaching in New York City. A woman came to my talk, and after the teaching, she approached me. Her body was emaciated. She was trembling. Basically you could tell that she was going through a very hard time. She told me that she had lived in an ashram in India for almost ten years. She had a guru. For a long time, she felt bliss every day and joy in the presence of her guru. Somehow there was a falling out between her guru and herself, and she was devastated. She lost all her joy, all her bliss. She ended up being disappointed and angry. So this is an example that sometimes we try to actualize those beautiful illusions of security in a spiritual world. There is no real happiness in trying to achieve or even in the notion that we already have those things that we long for—security and certainty.

My question is this: Have you ever really felt happiness, true happiness? This is a powerful question to ask. Of course, we may tell ourselves, "I remember feeling happiness many times." Or we may say, "I felt happiness ten years ago when I was on my honeymoon. That was true happiness, even though it didn't last a long time." Or "I remember that I felt happy when I won the lottery three years ago. That was true happiness, except it didn't last for more than a few weeks." My question again: Have you ever felt true happiness in your life, happiness that did not arise from any form of glory, success, gain, achievement, security, or comfort?

True happiness comes from a very strange reality, from loving uncertainty, from falling in love with the lack of security. Once you know how to love this truth, you are going to feel true happiness. You're going to know what true joy is. Then bliss is literally going to dance in your heart. Of course, the people around you are going to have difficulty understanding your bliss. That's OK. Then you are going to lose all your fear because there is nothing to be afraid of. Once the fear begins to dissolve, your heart is going to be filled with love. What can be more amazing than that? This is what Longchenpa and many other great masters have been trying to express all along. Everything becomes your friend. Everything becomes your friend, including unfavorable conditions such as separation, illness, and loss. Life becomes your friend. Nothing frightens you. No matter what happens in your life, you feel that everything is literally your friend. You feel that this life is your friend; this universe is your home. You are not afraid that the universe is a land of strangers where you always have to be cautious, paranoid, and defensive or offensive. You can open your heart and love this universe. You can dance with it.

CHAPTER SIX

# The Footprint of an Elephant

THERE ARE FOUR STAGES OF HUMAN LIFE: BIRTH, ILLNESS, old age, and death. These four stages are universal and also inevitable. Most human beings go through these four inevitable stages of life. Unfortunately, people sometimes don't have the opportunity to experience old age because they die too young. Those of us who think we are old should be very happy. Old age is a gift. It is a blessing that many people never have a chance to taste. Many people die from illness, hunger, and violence at an early age, before they have a chance to complete their life journey.

As you know, we all love birth, even though we don't remember our own. I'm sure some of you have parents who have videotapes and pictures of your birth. Aside from photos like these, we cannot recall our birth, but we all love it. We have birthday parties and invite all our loved ones. Everybody tries to have beautiful smiles on their faces. They bring gifts and poems. They make you feel like you are truly unique and special. They make you feel that you are some kind of shooting star that accidently landed on this world, some kind of angel. Of course, we are all amazing angels in some sense. We are all beautiful entities. The universe is manifesting itself through us, so we are, from that point of view, angels and shooting stars.

Then there is illness, which happens at quite an early age for many people. Therefore it is a topic that we cannot keep taboo. We look around and find that many people in our close proximity have an illness. We may find that some of our relatives or family members are sick right now. If they don't have a terminal illness, they may have a chronic disease. Because of that, we cannot keep illness a hidden topic, a taboo. Life forces us to discuss and talk about illness. I'm sure that many of us have already been seriously ill at some time in our lives. We all understand illness as, once again, an inevitable stage of this human life, and there are many profound spiritual teachings on how to deal with illness. There are many books written on it.

Perhaps the most meaningful topic to illuminate is death. We don't talk much about death in our everyday lives. Death is regarded as taboo most of the time. Not only that, there is a tremendous sense of fear regarding our own mortality, so we try everything in our power to deflect our attention away from that issue. We keep ourselves busy. We entertain ourselves to make sure that we remain oblivious to death and particularly to our own mortality. Yet the fear of death remains. Many great masters of the past said that the fear of death is a form of *mara,* a demon, one that lives in each of us. A powerful demon that has a kind of black magic that can put a spell on us. Sometimes it can ruin our happiness, and sometimes it can ruin our lives, ruin all of our opportunities or chances. We have many chances. We have the chance to become awakened. We have a chance to go inside and become the embodiment of love and wisdom. Yet that demon that is stopping us is not some kind of independent entity. It is a part of us, part of our psyche.

There is a paradox. We are very afraid of death, and we don't want to talk too much about it, especially when we are throwing a wonderful party, serving delicious cuisine, playing music, and lighting candles. In the midst of this, one topic we don't want to talk about is death. On the other hand, we are fascinated by death. We watch violent movies and get pleasure from death and from seeing people being killed. We also have plays and dramas in which there is much death—not just death, but very violent death. Some of us are fascinated with this form of entertainment. As you know, early in the twentieth century, an American named Walter Evans-Wentz translated an amazing book titled *The Tibetan Book of the Dead: Or After Death Experiences on the Bardo Plane*. It is a revolutionary book illuminating the process of dying and death. When Evans-Wentz translated that book, it became very popular, and many people in the West became fascinated with it. So we are very fascinated with death from one perspective, and at the same time we don't want to talk about death, especially our own death, at all. Maybe we don't mind talking about the death of others, but that does not apply to our own. We may discuss death, but we discuss it as some kind of objective, philosophical topic, not as a relevant, personal issue.

Buddha said that there are many meditations, yet the king of all meditations is the meditation on impermanence. He said there are many footprints, yet the footprint of the elephant is the most supreme. By this, Buddha was saying that the contemplation on impermanence is the most important and the most transformative meditation. It is the meditation we should not avoid, the meditation we should invite at some point in our lives. Sometimes when we are young and healthy, we do not think there is any purpose or even relevance in meditating on topics like impermanence, death, and dying. In our ordinary society, one of the best praises you can give someone is to say, "You look very young." Sometimes people ask you your age, but most of the time they don't. It is considered a very personal matter. Someone told me when I came to this country that I should not ask people their age. But if you do ask, you should say, "Oh. You look much younger than that." We all like to think that we are young and healthy. Imagine that you are really young, say in your twenties or thirties. You may think the idea of meditating on death and dying is not relevant to you. You may think, "This is spirituality for my grandparents or my old mother but not for me."

Of course, death is very difficult to accept. We are all afraid of it because it is unknown. Not only is it unknown, but there is also a belief that death is the end of everything, the end of our existence. Death, then, is the moment in which we are going to lose everything we cherish. We are never again going to have Christmas with our children. We are never again going to have a chance to see our favorite TV series, and we are never again going to eat our favorite chocolate. This is why it can be very frightening. Yet death is just part of the life cycle, as birth is. If you think of life as having its own seasons and cycles, then death would be like winter. Many people don't like winter. It is the time when all the trees lose their leaves and become brown and dry. There are no more flowers. But winter can be quite magical, especially around Christmas. Children get excited about Christmas. There is a lot of excitement that pretty much extends through the entire winter. Children are happy and waiting for Santa Claus to come from the North Pole, which is supposed to be a very snowy country with an abundance of gifts. Every time children think of it, their hearts are filled with joy. People decorate their trees, in the evening the lights reflect on the snow, and the whole winter becomes magical.

The point is that Buddha invited all of us to meditate on impermanence and especially on our own death and dying. This is not about whether you are dying or not or whether you are old or not. There is a whole different purpose behind it. Meditating on death—not just death as a concept, but your own death—is more than making preparations for death. Many of you are too young to prepare for death. You don't have to write your will yet. The point of meditating on death is not so much that you are making these preparations—writing your will, deciding who is going to inherit your money or your pillow or your car or your bed. It is more about realizing that you can die at any given moment.

One time this young woman came to my teaching. She looked very young and healthy. A few months after that, I was asked to do a prayer for someone who had just died. It turned out to be the woman who had come to my teaching only a few months before. She had died while swimming in the ocean. No matter how young or how healthy we are, there is no certainty that we are going to live another day. Most probably we are going to live a very long time, but we have to take into consideration this reality that we can die at any given moment. At the very least, we will come to the powerful realization that someday we are going to die. If not tomorrow, then someday we are going to die. We are totally mortal. We are not immortal. Of course, we all know that we are mortal. Nobody has the illusion that they are immortal. We kind of know that we are going to die. But have you ever felt the realization that you are going to die in your heart? Not just had some kind of theoretical understanding of it. Have you ever taken this contemplation that someday you are going to die into your heart, your bones, your marrow? When you do, you may feel fear, or your body may start trembling. So there is a fear that we have been avoiding. It doesn't matter whether you are going to die tomorrow or fifty years from now. There is this raw fear, this living, vibrant fear inside us when we truly contemplate our own death.

In the monasteries in Tibet, we are asked to contemplate our own death again and again, month after month. Soon you feel this fear. The point, once again, is to not run away from the fear but to live with it, to become more and more conscious of that fear, and to not even try to transform it. You don't have to live with that fear every moment, but you do have to become friendly with it and never fall into forgetfulness or denial—denial of your own death. Soon you will discover that the fear of death actually becomes a teaching, a true, authentic spirituality. That fear becomes the source of a profound understanding; you realize how precious this human life is. You begin to truly love this human life, realizing that it is precious because it can disappear at any moment. You begin to love everyday life from morning until evening. You realize that you are the richest person on the planet. The truth is that every person is the richest person on the planet. Every woman is the richest woman, every man is the richest man, simply by having this precious human life.

With that recognition of the preciousness of human life, you also begin to lose your fascination with superficial values. Instead, you know how to turn your attention toward the more profound and meaningful values of human life. Usually we tend to worship the superficial values in life. We tend to care too much about how much money we have in the bank or how we look. Or we are lost in our conventional achievements. Not only that, we become a little self-centered and selfish. Consult yourself. Ask yourself how much you are attached to conventional values that are superficial. Sometimes people worry too much about how they look. One of the most successful business industries these days is plastic surgery. People spend billions and billions of dollars on this. We also worry too much about our achievements and our social status. The consequence of worshipping these superficial values is suffering and misery. So with the recognition of our own mortality and the preciousness of this life, we begin to understand the more profound purpose of this existence, which is to love this life from morning until evening, to love this world, to love humanity, to have more compassion in this life, to help others, and to not hold on to hatred and anger.

I used to give this exercise to many people. I asked them to mark a date on their calendar as a day of experimentation, a day of contemplation. The idea is that on that day you meditate on your own mortality. You tell yourself to live that day as if it were the last day of your life. If you thought today was the last day you were going to live, what would you do? Perhaps you would pay more attention to the people around you. Maybe you would decide to give your full attention to your loved ones, your children. Maybe you would sacrifice your favorite TV show on that day and spend time with your children, hearing their laughter, looking into their faces and seeing their smiles, their wonder, and their magic. Or you might like to spend time with one of your friends and instead of judging him or her, you may be able to let go of your ego and be completely there for your friend, to love that person and show your utter reverence for him or her in each and every moment. You definitely wouldn't be worrying about your hairstyle. You might want to do something truly meaningful. Maybe you hurt somebody a long time ago, and you forgot to apologize. You might pick up the phone or write an e-mail and say, "I'm truly sorry I hurt you." Or you might be able to forgive somebody who harmed you at some time in your life. Or you might be able to write a check and offer a gift to those who are sick and vulnerable. Or you might be able to go outside and realize how beautiful and magical this world is. You might know how to be intoxicated by the bliss and ecstasy of falling in love with the universe. You might be able to enjoy every bite of food at the dinner table. This is how we should live each and every day. In the end, living a hundred years is the same as living one day. There is no difference.

Death is not frightening in the end. Neither is life. Many of the great masters wrote death poems. They wrote very inspiring poems before they died. Some say the whole dying process is like falling asleep at night. Are you afraid of falling asleep at night? Birth is like waking up in the early morning. Death is like falling asleep in the evening when your thoughts begin to subside, your sensory organs shut themselves down, and there is a deep peace. Death is like that. There is nothing to be afraid of in death.

Those great masters said they were going back to the *dharmakaya,* which in Buddhist terminology means the Supreme Source. For them, death was not this evil, existential ending. For them, death was not the end of everything. For them, death was going back. It was returning home to the Supreme Source. I know many people may be wondering what this Supreme Source is. It is just another way of naming the universe. You are going back into the universe. You are the universe, but you are also the play of the universe. The universe is manifesting, manifesting as you, and when you die, you dissolve back into the universe. The universe is always dancing, manifesting itself in myriad expressions. Then all of the expressions dissolve into the universe and manifest again. It is an eternal play. You are part of that eternal play. So you are the universe in the end. You are everything from that point of view. You are the stars in the sky. You are the trees in the forest. You are the Milky Way. You are also all the things in the landfill. Of course, you are all the beautiful, exotic flowers in the garden as well.

# CHAPTER SEVEN

# Love That Embraces Everything

At some point in our lives, we become self-conscious; we start perceiving that we are human beings in a giant universe. As time goes by, we have our own individuality, preferences, and memories as well as fantasies. Sometimes we feel that it's a gift from the universe to be a human being. We feel openhearted, ecstatic, and joyous. Other times we feel that it is very difficult to be a human being, especially when we get upset, despondent, or hopeless. Now and then we feel that we have a purpose in this human life, especially when we are able to do something that is rewarding. We don't have to build huge castles or an impressive monument to feel we have a purpose in this existence. We can feel there is a purpose to why we are here from simply writing a poem or composing music. Other times we may feel that we are very insignificant. We can feel like we are tiny insects holding on to a stick carried wildly in an endless cascading river.

Everybody feels that they are special at their birthday party. That is why so many people are attached to birthday parties. A party is one of those moments when we get a lot of attention. People feel that the whole universe is paying attention to them. Perhaps we all feel that we are significant rather than insignificant at this time. We feel that we are loved. We are recognized, and our existence is cherished by others. It's a reason why people sometimes get a little neurotic about their birthday parties. At a party, we receive lots of gifts and beautiful cards. When we read the cards, people say they are so happy that we are on this earth. So we feel that our existence is truly cherished, loved by others. Each of us is an individual and somehow an entity that is constantly unfolding.

You may be able to feel this entity right now, the one who is breathing, feeling the heartbeat, hearing the sound. This is your own individual entity. As I said earlier, now and again we feel this entity, and it is truly amazing, marvelous, and significant. Other times we feel that this entity is just meaningless, unloved, and uncherished. Such perceptions can cause us pain or even depression. Some of us may be able to go back and remember the beginning of this entity. Some of us may have become self-conscious at a very early age. Some people claim that they remember the ancient beginning of their being. Most people remember the beginning of their being at the age of three or four but not much earlier than that. At the same time, even though there is this entity, there is no independent and singular self in that entity. There is obviously an entity. We have memories. We were somewhere yesterday. We may remember many events that have happened in our lives—pleasant events that we want to recall as well as many unpleasant events. This morning you woke up, you brushed your teeth, and now you are here. So there is this continuation in the entity of your being. Yet when you look carefully, there is no singular self. Buddhist traditions teach that we are composed of five aggregates, and perhaps we are made of those five aggregates. So we are this amazing gathering. A mandala is a sacred realm. How about if we call ourselves mandalas? That is much more poetic instead of regarding ourselves as a kind of mishmash made out of many components. Let's each try to regard ourselves as a mandala, a sacred dimension that is made up of many sacred components. So we are this living, intricate mandala. Because of that, we are ready to fall apart. If there were a singular self, then we wouldn't fall apart. But because we are this living mandala made of so many components, more than five aggregates in my understanding, we are ready to fall apart at any given moment. We are ready to fall apart outwardly as well as inwardly. Our existence is always ready to disappear. This mandala, which is who you are, is truly beautiful but also truly fragile, way more fragile than you think. All I can say is that we are truly beautiful but extremely fragile. Please remember that we are ready to fall apart at any given moment. This mandala, this sacred universe, which is who we are, is always ready to fall apart. This realization—knowing that there is no singular self in each of us, and instead we are this complex, beautiful, living mandala—is very liberating. It can give rise to courage, love, and joy in our hearts.

I was visiting a Zen Buddhist monastery recently. I met with these three monks who get up at four o'clock every morning and meditate the whole day. One monk has been meditating for ten years from morning until evening—truly impressive. They welcomed me and had tea with me. They were very curious about me, and finally they shared some kind of candy bar with me. One man asked me why the factories made such candy bars and why they put the wrappers on the candy. He asked me a series of questions. I answered him. I told him that this can be explained by very old Buddhist logic, a Buddhist view called *pratityasamutpada* (interdependence). Everything comes into being through causes and conditions. Even a candy bar comes into being through many causes and conditions. Some of them can be explained; some of them are beyond my comprehension. Then this Zen monk said, "Your answer is not a correct answer. But I understand that the answer is the Tibetan way. But we don't answer this way. We would say something like three plus three is nine." Then he told me that they have a method to check out whether somebody has deep realization or not, whether somebody has insight or not. They never told me whether they approved of my insight or not because I never worried about whether I had insight or not. You see, there are people in this world who worry even more than I do about whether I have insight or not.

In some sense, both answers are right. My answer, which is the Tibetan Buddhist way, is right. The Zen answer is also right. The Tibetan Buddhist answer is right because, as a human being, each of us is this amazing mandala that comes into being through many causes and conditions. We are made of many sacred components, many aggregates—consciousness, body, bones, flesh, and marrow. We can comprehend that. But there are things that we cannot comprehend, such as subtle body and subtle mind. There is a subtle body in each of us, but we are not aware of it most of the time unless we immerse ourselves in awareness and deep reflection. Then we begin to be aware of a whole new dimension of the body. They call it subtle body. Tantric Buddhism has perhaps the most advanced understanding of the human subtle body. The human subtle body is not the field of our conditioned mind, our coarse mind. The coarse mind is only aware of the coarse level of the body. We can feel our bodies, we can touch our feet, we can look at our faces in the mirror. But that is only the coarse level of our own bodies. There is a whole subtle energetic body in each of us. That is why those beautiful, ancient Tantric teachings developed symbols and language. They came up with the signs for the chakras, *pranas,* and *bindus* in order to describe the human subtle body. There is even subtle mind. Once again, the conditioned mind is not aware of subtle mind. The conditioned mind is not aware of many of our own sacred components. So once again, each of us is this amazing, intricate, truly marvelous, living mandala—a mandala with many sacred components. Each person is like a lotus with millions of petals, like a diamond with trillions of facets. How amazing we are.

So we are neither good nor bad. This sacred mandala, this living mandala that is your being, came into existence through many countless noble and ordinary causes and conditions. So Tibetan Buddhists are absolutely right. But that Zen monk is also right. Ultimately we don't understand who we are. We are each a great mystery. We never understand who we are and why we are here. We never understand where we are coming from and where we are going. So we have to let go of all our comprehension. We may have to let go of our minds sometimes to surrender to that great mystery of our own entity, our own beingness. From that point of view, we are neither good nor bad. We are neither loveable nor unloveable. We are neither perfect nor imperfect. All of this experience that we go through every day—liking ourselves, not liking ourselves—is just our mental play. Those experiences have nothing to do with who we are. We are neither significant nor insignificant. All I can say is that this amazing entity, this living mandala, is like a river. Sometimes it freezes; other times it flows gracefully. Usually love melts your being, and fear freezes your being. So love and fear are the two most powerful experiences you can have. In other words, you can say that almost all of your experiences one way or another can be categorized as love or fear. There is a fear in each of us, the fear of falling apart, the fear of this existence falling apart. That fear turns into insecurity. That insecurity sometimes becomes violence, anger, hatred, and doubt. That fear serves as the ground for all of our neuroses.

Then love melts us. Sometimes love has an object—our children, this world, or ourselves. There is also love without an object. Some people call it divine love. It is the highest level of love, love without an object. When we feel that love, our entire being becomes that love, and the channels in our bodies begin to open. We have to bring our bodies into our spirituality. The body should not be rejected. Enlightenment, transformation, healing, whatever we are aspiring to, we cannot experience any of them without bringing the body into spirituality. So there is healing in the body; there is enlightenment in the body. We cannot be healed without healing the body. When we become that divine love, the body literally begins to melt; the channels, the chakras within it, begin to open; and we feel more love, more courage. When we feel this divine love, the mind begins to melt, and it undoes all the knots inside it. There is a large mass of knots in the mind; our belief systems and the thought patterns that we are so attached to are the knots in our minds. Those knots bind, imprison, and torment us. They take freedom and peace away from us. This love that I am speaking about is a pure experience of melting our frozen hearts and our knotted minds.

This true love is not the feeling of oneness, the feeling that we are one with the universe. True love embraces everything; it does not reject anything. This love that I am speaking about is something we can cultivate. There are many methodologies to cultivate this love. There are beautiful songs we can sing. There are profound verses we can recite. There are meditations we can practice as a means to cultivate this love. Sooner or later, we feel that we become this pure love, this objectless love. Buddha became this objectless love. He is always love. So the very quintessence of this living mandala of your self is pure love. The quintessence of your being is pure love. The nature of the river is this beautiful flow, even though it sometimes freezes. To truly realize that the very quintessence of your being is true love, you may have to have self-knowledge, which is this honest and complete understanding of yourself. It is being aware of your divinity as well as your limitations. You already know that you have divinity, and you know that you have courage and love. You know that you are generous and openhearted. You also know that sometimes you are able to give of yourself for the well-being of everyone else. It won't be difficult for you to love your own holiness. At the same time, you have limitations—fear, insecurity, and selfishness. Once you become aware of these limitations, don't try to demonize or condemn them. If you demonize your imperfections, then you may end up being more and more frozen.

Once you become aware of your coarse neuroses as well as your subtle neuroses, love them. Love all your neuroses. Love all your imperfections. Learn to love your fear and your anger as well. Always be aware of them, and they will dissolve on their own. They will keep dissolving by themselves without any effort. As time goes by, you become more and more this melting, living mandala rather than this frozen one. Your heart is filled with more joy and more love. You feel more and more connected to this world as a paradise—an imperfect paradise, not a perfect paradise. In the end, you may love everyone and everything that exists.

CHAPTER EIGHT

# A Thorn Lodged in the Heart

IMAGINE THAT YOU WERE RAISED IN THE DESERT OR IN A jungle by animals. Animals cared for you and fed you exotic foods. Imagine that you never saw human beings in your life. I'm sure you would have some problems like being thirsty and hungry, but perhaps you would also have some of the human feelings such as fear, anxiety, jealousy, or resentment. It is very interesting to be part of this human family. We can learn how to love each other. We can experience intimacy, connection, and resolution with each other. At the same time, many of our internal conflicts arise from being part of this family. We all have conflict inside that has to do with our relationship with others.

Recently I was leading a weeklong meditation retreat. Every day I spoke with a group of people, and I also met with individuals. People felt very safe sharing their innermost secrets, their wounds, and their pain with me. They poured out everything in front of me. There is power in sharing and voicing what has been hidden.

Amazingly, I learned that most of the time our pain and suffering originates out of our relationships with other human beings. It starts with our parents and other people who were close to us when we were young. Out of our experiences with other human beings, we feel hatred, resentment, and jealousy. We compare ourselves with others, sometimes feeling pride and other times feeling guilt, shame, and self-loathing. If we look inside, we can see that we all have wounds, pain, suffering, and self-loathing to a certain extent. They all come from our relationship with this human world. Sometimes we are not in touch with any internal conflict. We are not in touch with our own pain, anger, and self-loathing.

In one of his teachings, Buddha said that seeing people locked in conflict made him completely distraught. But on close examination, he discerned a thorn, hard to see, lodged deep in their hearts. Buddha felt distraught seeing people locked in conflict, and we see that too, right now in our own time. There is a lot of war happening in the world, and we cannot turn our attention away from it. There is also violence and injustice and an unbelievable amount of both physical and mental suffering. Therefore it is totally understandable to sometimes feel distraught or hopeless. Sometimes we are thinking about our human brothers and sisters who live on the other side of the world. We also see suffering in our own families and in ourselves. Remember, Buddha said that when he looked, he saw a thorn. It is a very powerful simile, a thorn. He said a thorn is lodged in our hearts. He also said that it is very hard to see. There are lots of thorns lodged in our hearts. They are hard to see unless we pay attention, unless we quiet our minds and turn our attention completely inward to hear the cry of our hearts and the confusion of our minds. Perhaps you recognize that there is a thorn inside you, a thorn of anger or resentment.

With this in mind, I would like to share a beautiful practice on forgiveness. This spiritual practice will benefit all of us. Forgiveness can set our hearts free. It can remove the thorn from our hearts. If we don't know how to forgive, then we will be walking around for the rest of our lives with that thorn lodged in our hearts. Even if we are not aware of it, we feel the pain coming from it, and that pain will influence and color all aspects of our lives. It will color our relationships with people and with the world as well. When I look into my own heart, I have found that there is great reason for me to practice forgiveness. I realize that I have many people in my life that I have to forgive. This is a beautiful epiphany. It is not a negative or disheartening realization. As a Tibetan person, I realize that I have to forgive many people in this life. The idea of forgiveness is much more liberating than holding on to resentment and anger. In the same way, when you look into yourself, if you look with complete honesty and courage, you may find many of these thorns. You may find that there are whole groups of people you have to forgive that you haven't forgiven yet. You may have to forgive your parents, your relatives, your friends, or humanity. You may have to forgive the world of men as well as the world of women. Or you may have to forgive yourself. And definitely you have to forgive humanity, because humans have been very destructive toward each other.

But forgiveness is not really easy. It is especially not easy to truly forgive when there is no divine or eternal reward. Here I am saying that there is no divine or eternal reward if you forgive, yet it can be the most liberating experience you can ever witness. Forgiveness comes from understanding the human condition and understanding where each of us is coming from. Understanding those who have caused harm to us. Understanding their karma, their background, their suffering, their delusions and realizing that there is no evil in anybody. There is no evil in human beings. Ultimately, nobody hurts anyone else intentionally, even though we may sometimes feel that we have been hurt intentionally. Everyone is harming each other with complete unawareness. So we are ruled by our own delusions, our own neuroses. Sometimes all we need is this understanding. When we have this understanding, there is no human being in this world we cannot forgive. Imagine you are looking into the heart of another, and you can see that heart is full of wounds. Imagine you are looking into the mind, the consciousness of another, and you recognize that there is a cloud, a cloud of confusion. As long as we are walking around with this thorn in our hearts, we will always be in pain. We will be suffering secretly and silently. We may not be aware of our own pain. We will still, of course, go to parties, eat delicious food, and play music. We will be busy with our daily chores, and yet there will be silent pain.

I would like to ask all of you to keep going inside and to keep inquiring until you find all these old thorns. Remember, Buddha reminded us that they are not easy to see. If you can let go of some of these thorns, you will experience indescribable freedom and joy, as expressed by many of the ancient masters, especially the Zen masters. Wumen Huikai, a famous Chan master wrote this poem:

Ten thousand flowers in spring.
The moon in autumn.
The cool breeze in summer.
Snow in winter.
If your mind is not clouded by all of these unnecessary things,
This is the best season of your life.


Are you experiencing the best season of your life? Do you experience this every day? Every morning? Every afternoon? Every evening? Do you know how to let your heart get drunk with joy and bliss? Do you have a clear recollection that yesterday your heart was drunk with bliss? Do you remember a time this week when your heart was drunk with bliss for no reason? Have you felt pure joy, pure love, and pure freedom at least once sometime within the last ten days? If you can forgive everybody, including yourself, you may be able to feel this joy, this unconditional freedom. You may feel that every day is the best season of your life. When there are no more thorns in your heart, then perhaps the only thing you experience is this pure joy all the time. You will be falling in love in each moment. You will be falling in love with everything, with nature and with all of these countless wonders manifesting every moment.

One time a scholar went to see the Zen master Ryokan, who lived in a hermitage. The two spent hours and hours together and talked about philosophy, literature, art, and poetry. At one point, Ryokan told the scholar that he was going to go out for some sake, a traditional Japanese liquor. He said, "When I return, we can continue our delightful conversation." The Zen master left. Hours and hours went by, and he didn't return. The scholar thought that maybe something terrible had happened to him, so he went looking for him. Just outside the hermitage, he found Ryokan sitting completely amused by the moon. The scholar said, "You have been gone for hours and hours. Do you realize that? I was afraid something terrible had happened to you." The Zen master spoke calmly, "You have come here at just the right moment. Look into the sky. How splendid the moon is." The scholar said, "Yes, the moon is very splendid, but where is the sake?" Ryokan said, "Oh yes, the sake. Sorry, I forgot. I'm going to get some for you." And he got up and left. The scholar was amused and confused.

Perhaps we can experience the consciousness of this great Zen master. We may feel completely enchanted by everything from morning until evening if we can let go of all the thorns in our hearts. Of course, there is a time to be angry. I am not saying you should never be angry. There is a time to have grief, sadness, and anger. Yet maybe there are also unnecessary things that we are holding on to right now. We can hold on to anger and resentment for a long time. Can we let go of it? This question, and others like it, can be very powerful. They can be regarded as spiritual practice. Of course, the question has to be asked at the right moment. Sometimes when there is readiness and openness, all you have to do is ask yourself this powerful question. You may be shocked to find that you are ready to let go of your pain and your sorrow. Maybe you are able to let go of a thorn that you have been carrying for many decades. You can let go of the burden in a single moment.

Perhaps you can start by forgiving yourself. Forgiving yourself is a form of empowerment. It is a true *abhisheka*. *Abhisheka* is a Tantric ceremony of empowerment. It's the ceremony of empowering yourself as the ultimate Buddha, empowering yourself as Avalokiteshvara or Tara. There is no Tantric master bestowing this empowerment on you. You give this empowerment to yourself. When you totally forgive yourself, you know how to accept yourself. Then you will love yourself madly. You'll give this empowerment to yourself. Then you will be enthroning yourself as Avalokiteshvara, the embodiment of infinite love. You'll be enthroning yourself as Tara, the embodiment of boundless compassion.

CHAPTER NINE

# A Very Old Secret

Not long ago, someone from Germany told me that she came all the way to the United States to meet with a Tibetan lama. As it turned out, he was a friend of mine. He passed away quite a while ago. She came to see this lama to find answers to life's important questions. She had a lot of high expectations. My friend looked quite exotic. He had a turban and wore exotic clothes. She told me that one day he asked her, "Are you having fun?" The question challenged her mind because that question is not very profound. She thought, "He's too Californian." So there is a rumor going around in this world that Californians are only into having fun. Of course, when he asked that question, he was not asking if she was having fun in a casual sense. He was asking this question from a totally different point of view. Many people, especially spiritual seekers, are not interested in just having fun. Many of them are looking for grand, lofty notions such as absolute nirvana. As you know, there are many conflicting theories about nirvana itself, which is not good news. Some say that nirvana is an eternal achievement that goes on forever once you have it, like the sky it remains forever. Some say that nirvana is an epiphany that you can experience now and then. These are two conflicting theories of nirvana. Many people are looking for nirvana as more of an eternal achievement. Many people are dedicating a lot of effort trying to achieve that. I'm not denying the existence of such eternal achievement. Please don't misunderstand me. All I am saying is that there seem to be a lot of theories about nirvana. I am not sure how many of you are searching for nirvana. It seems that the younger generation is not too interested in looking for it. But if you go east you will find, even today, many individuals making incredible spiritual endeavors trying to achieve not only nirvana, but nirvana as an eternal achievement, the same as being in union with Brahman, the eternal union with the divine.

I am not going to talk about nirvana as an eternal achievement or even as some kind of holy epiphany. My friend, this wonderful Tibetan lama who passed away, had a special gift. He had this gift of cutting through the trappings of a lot of fancy words and fancy concepts. He would say something so simple, so human, and yet it made total sense. Just like this question, "Are you having fun?" I am presenting this question to you. Are you having fun? Most people in this world are not having fun. Having fun here does not mean having fun by getting drunk and being a party animal. It does not mean delving into sensual pleasure and dangerous sport. It's more than that, even though the language sounds so casual, so Californian. Most people are feeling heaviness in their hearts, a sense of drudgery regarding everyday life. They are not finding any joy, vibrancy, or sense of sacredness in their everyday lives. It seems that this drudgery of everyday life is defined by repetitive tasks like cooking food, making beds, mowing the lawn, going to the same office, and having the same kind of thinking process. Think about cleaning the house, sweeping the floor with a broom. Can you imagine that you could find great joy just sweeping the floor? Can you imagine singing a song to yourself while sweeping the floor and dancing with the broom? Not too many people dance with a broom. It would be wonderful to dance with a broom. Isn't that a lovely image—dancing instead of feeling drudgery and meaninglessness? Feeling a sense of sacredness, wonder, and devotion in an ordinary chore like sweeping the floor and then dancing and singing with the broom?

Many people feel that they don't want to be in this body. Do you have the experience periodically that you want to get out of your body? Have you experienced not feeling comfort and harmony with your body? Have you experienced having pain and anger stored in your body, feeling that this body is an encumbrance, drudgery, a burden? Do you feel that having this human incarnation is a drain? Of course, when you go through challenges like health issues and old age, it is quite rational to feel the cumbersomeness of having a human body. But even without those challenges, some people still feel a silent suffering with their body. They do not feel joy and bliss in their being. In simple language, they are not having fun. So here, having fun means being able to enjoy yourself completely and enjoy being incarnated in this body. It means loving this life completely. Having that joy at the core of your being seems to be a bit unusual for most people. Imagine yourself as somebody who

[ 79 ]

dances with a broom. People will find this very strange. If you were running for political office, perhaps you would never get elected. Your opponents would go around showing pictures of you dancing with a broom, and people would think you are too sweet, innocent. You would never get elected.

"Are you having fun?" is a powerful question to ask. In some traditions, the master asks the disciple questions. Here I am not playing the role of the master with you as my disciple. But I am asking if you are having fun. Are you feeling harmony and genuine peace being incarnated in this body? Are you feeling that this world, this universe is already paradise? Are you feeling that your body is a sanctuary, a temple where you like to be? Are you feeling that your body is the temple where you want to stay, where you want to open your heart, where you want to dance, where you want to sing songs, where you feel that you are embraced by sacredness and grace? Many ancient Buddhist masters have said that this world is Akanishta paradise, the highest paradise. Not only is this world paradise, it is the highest of all paradises. Are you feeling like you are living in the highest paradise? If you know how to have fun, then you may feel, sooner or later, that your body is a sacred temple. And you may feel that this world is the highest paradise. But first you have to know how to have fun. Forget about nirvana for a while and learn how to have fun.

These days when people come to see me, they don't ask me questions about nirvana. They often talk about what they are going through, whether they are sitting in a mediation retreat or in their homes. They like to talk about their experience. They often talk about being contracted, about being narrowed inside. Many people are hoping they can experience the opposite of that. They hope they can experience a sense of being spacious, open, and expansive inside. Once we are contracted inside, we don't know how to have fun. But once we are melting inside and being spacious, we know how to have fun. Then we know how to experience the pure joy that comes from realizing and experiencing that our bodies, our beings, are sacred temples and the universe is the highest paradise. I would like to ask you to go inside and find out whether or not you are contracted inside. The state of being contracted can be called samsara. The state of being totally melted can be called nirvana.

Now you may be wondering if there is some kind of secret that allows us to unfreeze ourselves, to melt, to become spacious and expansive inside. There is a secret, but the secret is not new. It's a very old secret. The secret is the wisdom of nongrasping. As you know, there is this idea of *mara* in the East. You'll find this notion of *mara* in almost every teaching in the East. *Mara* literally means the "killer," the "executioner." *Mara* in a contemporary way means a force that messes up your life and does not allow you to have fun. That is how I interpret *mara*. It is not so much a dark force that casts a spell on you and sends you into some kind of scary realm. Rather it is a force that somehow freezes you inside and doesn't allow you to have fun. This *mara* is in each of us.

In the Chöd lineage of Tibetan Buddhism, there are four *maras,* the four obstructing forces. They are the demon of attachment to form, the demon of attachment to formlessness, the demon of attachment to joy, and the demon of attachment to conceit. Grasping is like a demon. Here the demon is only an analogy. We are not speaking of literal demons. Usually a demon is a force that follows you all the time, like a shadow from which you cannot escape. Sometimes you feel that it is a part of you, and at other times you feel that it is separate from you. But it always follows you, no matter where you go. If you go to a party, it follows you. If you go into a cave to meditate, it follows you. Yet, you will not find its home. That's what a demon is. But here the demon is not outside. Demon is only a metaphor.

So your tendency toward grasping is like a demon. It always follows you like a shadow. It imprisons you. It binds you; it binds you to suffering. In this analogy, the first demon is grasping forms. It is our attachment to forms such as our possessions, our houses, our wealth, our clothing, our cars, and also our relationships. We can be very attached to our possessions. We can be so attached that we identify with them. Our possessions become another extension of ourselves. This is why we say, "my house," "my car," and "my bank account." Imagine that you are going through a midlife crisis, and you want to buy a smashing sports car. Then suddenly you feel that you are that car. You feel that you are so dashing: "Even though I am in my forties, look at me. I'm cool. I'm just totally dashing. I can go fast, and I can get lots of admiration from everybody." Many people here go through a midlife crisis. When you jump into a sports car, nobody sees you. They don't see your gray hair or the wrinkles popping up all over your face. You can hide all that, and suddenly you become this amazing, truly impressive being. Imagine that you park your car and go to a restaurant to celebrate. Then somebody accidently hits your car and makes a dent in it. When you come out, you see this dent and you totally fall apart. You feel that somebody has damaged your ego. Somebody created a dent in your self-image.

This is an example of how attached we are to our possessions. Our grasping becomes a demon. Our obsession with outside things becomes a demon. It freezes us inside. It makes us insecure. It makes us selfish. Let me clarify that I am not saying you should not enjoy having things in your life. You can enjoy having many beautiful things in life. You can have a nice car. There is nothing wrong with that. You can have a beautiful house. You can wear beautiful clothes. There is nothing wrong with that as long as you are not obsessed with them. As long as you are not using them to define who you are.

This is also true in the area of human relationships. There is nothing wrong with having relationships. There are many perspectives to human relationships. Relationships can be wonderful. For some people, relationships are a source of fellowship and comfort, as well as a spiritual path. It is a powerful spiritual journey when our beloved one becomes a mirror that reflects our darkness as well as our divinity. But when you are attached to your relationship, it becomes a demon. It binds you. It holds you back from evolving. It prevents you from growing. It becomes a very beautiful hindrance to the extent that you may never find out who you are in this life. You may substitute your relationship for self-knowledge and the process of acquiring self-knowledge, understanding yourself. In the end, you have to find yourself. To find yourself, you may need to be alone, not outwardly but inwardly. You'll find your darkness, and in the end, you'll find your divinity, your original face, the infinite within. But when you are grasping at outer relationships, you may never find this stance about yourself. So don't get attached to relationships.

The second demon is the demon of formlessness, which means our thoughts and emotions. They are formless. Our thoughts and emotions are not demons, but our obsession with them is; our grasping at them is a form of demon. It is the form of a shadow. This is different than trying to transcend or escape from our emotions. It is different than trying to control or transcend our thoughts. When you feel an emotion such as fear, the moment you grasp at it, something freezes inside you. Then suddenly you may feel that the universe is not a paradise but actually a very unfriendly world that you have to struggle and fight against. Even though you may not see any opponents in front of you, you feel you have to fight. You have to struggle. There is nothing you can do with fear. Fear is just part of human existence. Everyone has their own fears. Fear arises in the same way love and joy arise.

The secret of having fun is nongrasping. Once you know how to use the wisdom of nongrasping, you will really want to be in this human incarnation. You won't want to go anywhere. You may feel like you want to be here forever, and then some day you may be dancing with a broom. Dancing with a broom is very poetic. There are anecdotes about the ancient masters dancing with a broom. How about soon you will be dancing with a vacuum cleaner? People ask me from time to time to give them a spiritual practice. Now I am giving you a spiritual practice. Our *sadhana,* our spiritual practice, is very simple. I am giving you a spiritual secret, a spiritual practice, which is to dance with a vacuum cleaner. But make sure no one is videotaping you in case you wish to run for political office someday.

# CHAPTER TEN

# No Place to Land

HUMAN LIFE IS NOT ONLY PRECIOUS, IT IS ALSO EXTREMELY transient. We are not immortal. We can die at any given moment. And even if we are fortunate enough to live for another ten or twenty years, that is really not very long. Life is passing in front of our eyes. This understanding is quite valuable. It wakes us up and forces us to reflect and think about the purpose of this human life. I encourage you to take time now and reflect on this truth: the impermanent and ever-changing reality of human existence. It helps us let go of our attachment to all the unimportant things to which we give so much attention.

We are obsessed with many unimportant things. We pay attention to all these things that don't have any meaning. When we realize how fleeting and impermanent our own existence is, we wake up and feel an urgency to do something meaningful with our human lives. In Eastern traditions, when we have this feeling of emergency from realizing the impermanent nature of our human existence, we feel that we are ready to walk the spiritual path and realize nirvana. We end up thinking that the purpose of this life is to realize nirvana. These days, hardly anybody talks about nirvana, and there are some good reasons for that. For most people, it is not a very entertaining subject. In addition to that, there are all kinds of theories about nirvana. There is not one universal definition or understanding of nirvana. Some people think that nirvana is a kind of eternal achievement, a perfect place with no more suffering, no more misery, where we will be ecstatic forever. Nirvana is seen as a place that is completely disconnected from all worldly reality, a place rising above everything. That version of nirvana can sound abstract. Perhaps you haven't thought much about nirvana; maybe you have never even heard of the word. For someone like me, this notion of nirvana is very important. I have been using all my resources, all my energy, and all my heart since I was a child to achieve it. So for me, this is a big topic, something I cannot let go of because decades and decades of my life have been spent trying to achieve this thing called nirvana. I cannot let go of it easily. I want to find out exactly what it is.

Perhaps the goal of this human life is to realize nirvana, but perhaps nirvana is not what some people think it is. Nirvana does not have to be some kind of permanent, static, or eternal state of freedom or enlightenment. Instead, it can be alive and vibrant, something that can be actualized here and now. It can be experienced here, in our human bodies, in our flesh, in our bones. It can be felt in our relationship with the world, with humanity, with animals, and with nature. When we feel this nirvana, we feel only pure love and pure compassion. Love and compassion for ourselves and for all humanity, as well as love for animals and nature. Compassion is not dead; it is very much alive. We have many concepts of and even lots of fancy doctrines about love and compassion. However, most of them are not alive. They are dead. The only compassion and love that are alive are burning in our hearts. So nirvana must be alive, in the same way that true compassion and true love are totally alive. They are as alive as the blood circulating in our bodies. They are as vibrant as the beat of our hearts.

We can apply this very old model, this archetype called nirvana, as a way to understand where we are going and what the highest mission of our lives is. There is a type of practice in the Tibetan tradition known as *lojong* (mind training). *Lojong* was a new movement, a revolution in Tibetan Buddhism. This revolution can be attributed to the Indian master Atisha. It sounds like Atisha felt that many Tibetan Buddhists were missing the point. Perhaps he felt they were using all of these beautiful religious practices to escape from the true work, the inner work, the work of growing their hearts and expanding their ability to love, to forgive, and to accept. *Lojong* teachings have many profound verses and phrases that we can memorize. One of the most profound phrases suggests taking all the circumstances in life as the path, the path to the nirvana, the path to the great awakening. The idea is that we don't have to run away from any circumstances in our lives. Usually we are running away from many unfavorable situations. There is a whole list of conditions such as illness, loss, and failure. These conditions challenge our ego, sense of security, comfort, and even happiness. According to the *lojong* teachings, we don't have to run away from them. It says that we can welcome all the circumstances of life, even the unfavorable ones, and use them as a spiritual path, a path to nirvana, a path to the great awakening. By following that path, we can learn how to surrender, how to forgive, how to become courageous, and how to find happiness—not from outside, but from inside.

I travel frequently and meet with many people of different cultures. I keep running into very impressive, incredible people. They are like living bodhisattvas, spiritual heroes and heroines. I often find inspiring bodhisattvas among ordinary people. Many of these people have become who they are because they have suffered in their lives. Somehow they had the willingness to not run away from the suffering but to face it and use it as a path to awakening or a path of inner growth. They learned how to become courageous, how to have big minds and big hearts. If you are courageous, then somehow all of life is dharma; all of life is a spiritual teaching. You can almost say that everybody is your spiritual teacher, your guru. Some of those gurus are like Zen masters. They are sometimes a little difficult to hang around with. Many of them are eccentric and sometimes wrathful. They may hit you with a stick. In the same way, the circumstances of life are sometimes wrathful. The truth is that we have no control over life's circumstances. We already know this. From the moment we are born, we have no control over our own existence. We don't have the choice to be born in a certain time or to a particular family. We have no choice over where we are born. We don't choose to be born in a certain time, place, and to a certain family. In the same way, we have no control over our future. The future is completely unknown. I am not talking simply about what will unfold in the long-distant future. Even this evening is completely unknown, because there is no absolute certainty regarding what will unfold this evening. Most probably, we will wake up tomorrow morning, but there is no 100 percent guarantee that we will. This kind of profound understanding sometimes becomes vivid in our consciousness when we have a tragedy or a crisis in our lives, when we feel we are pushed to the edge of the unknown. But this profound insight does not come easily when we are feeling completely secure, enveloped in layers of glory, worldly success, and comfort. It comes about when we surrender completely to the unknown, the great unknown. It comes about when we learn to love this great unknown and when we realize that it is, indeed, the foundation of all existence. It is the foundation of our lives. Once we can surrender and love this great unknown, there is only freedom; there is only joy. Then we can let go of these long-held chains binding us inside: the chain of hope and the chain of fear. Then we can be the happiest people who ever lived on the planet. The secret of everything we are looking for—nirvana, enlightenment, the great awakening, or whatever we call it—is surrender.

What is it that we are looking for? Some of us know. We can say, "I am looking for nirvana." Some of us are already exhausted from looking for nirvana. If nirvana is not what you are looking for, then happiness might definitely be what you are looking for. We are all looking for happiness. Nirvana, enlightenment, liberation, they are just different ways of understanding the happiness we all long for. We are either looking for happiness on earth or happiness in heaven.

There is nothing wrong with having this longing. It is inborn in all of us. It is perhaps the strongest impulse we have.

Every living being in this universe, in the visible world and the invisible world, longs for happiness as its strongest impulse. But happiness cannot be achieved by accumulating and holding on to outside favorable circumstances and worldly glories. I don't know whether there is an eternal happiness or not, but there is an unconditional happiness. Unconditional happiness comes from this secret: surrender. Surrender is the act of loving and embracing the great unknown. Unconditional happiness comes from not running away from anything. It comes from taking even the most unfavorable circumstances as a path, a spiritual path, a truthful teaching. Surrender uses such circumstances as a way to turn our attention inward, as a way to see our limitations, our neuroses, laziness, cowardice, fear, insecurity, pride, and attachment. From that understanding, we grow and develop love, compassion, and courage. Life is unfolding continuously, whether we like it or not. The more we try to control it, the more we suffer. If we truly surrender our fears and hopes and jump into the unknown of everyday life, we'll lose nothing except suffering. We'll gain freedom without looking for it. A Tibetan master said, "The bad news is that you have to jump out of the plane without a parachute. The good news is that there is no place to land." He was talking about this secret.

There are many beautiful visualization practices in Tantric Buddhism, as well as in other spiritual traditions. To me, the most powerful visualization is this: visualize that you are losing everything and learn to surrender to that. Learn to be compassionate and content.

Learn to dance in your heart while in your mind you are losing everything. Learn not to become angry, bitter, or pessimistic. The truth is that we are going to lose everything in the end. It is just a matter of time. When death arises, then we have to lose everything. We cannot take even one object with us. We have to leave everything behind—this beautiful world, our loved ones, our friends, our fortune, our glory, and our physical bodies. There is now a message happening in all of us; this message is quite urgent. It is trying to wake us up. It is telling us that the purpose of this existence is to walk the spiritual path, the path to nirvana, the path to the great awakening. This message is also telling us, "Don't seek nirvana in the future, but find nirvana here, here in the nowness." It is the state you find yourself in after complete surrender.

# CHAPTER ELEVEN

# This Precious Gift

MANY PEOPLE IN THIS WORLD DO NOT HAVE THE OPPOR-
tunity or even the interest to explore the life of contemplation. They
are very busy and preoccupied by their mundane affairs, trying to
make a living, raising their children, participating in politics and
social affairs. Yet without contemplation, our lives remain quite
superficial. We may be missing the big picture. There are many
forms of reflection. Buddha started a meditation retreat known as
the monsoon retreat, where his students spent almost three months
in solitude and practiced reflection and contemplation. There are
people in the world even today who have completely left society
behind. They live in solitude in the monasteries to immerse themselves in the life of reflection. Of course, most of us don't have the
luxury to spend many years in the forest or in a monastery to practice
reflection. At the same time, we find many moments in everyday
life where we can pause, turn our attention inward, and practice
reflection that will make our lives richer.

There are two aspects of this human life: the exterior life and the interior life. Many people live only the exterior life and not the interior life. The truth is that the interior life is equally important as the exterior one. We all naturally live the exterior life, which is about going to school, finding a career, having a relationship, cooking food, going to parties, and so forth. Periodically we go out shopping, and we can spend the whole day doing nothing but shopping. Sometimes we don't even have to buy anything. We can go around just doing what we call window-shopping. This, along with making friends, is a big part of the exterior life.

Then there is the interior life. Many people haven't explored it. When we totally ignore living the interior life, then life becomes empty and shallow. That means we are not living our lives fully. Not only that, we begin feeling this silent pain and dissatisfaction as a consequence of ignoring the interior life. We already know there is some kind of universal suffering happening everywhere, suffering that we can manage most of the time. We can keep it silent. We can pretend not to be aware of it. It's not like suffering some kind of major crisis. When we have a major crisis, we cannot ignore it. When our house is on fire or a loved one is sick, we cannot ignore such suffering. But there is this ongoing suffering, a kind of under-lying pain, the pain of this human life, and this is the sense of "dissatisfactoriness." Somehow everyone is suffering from it, and it ultimately originates from ignoring the interior life. We can eat the best food in the world, we can amass a fortune, and we can travel to all the desirable destinations in this world. Now, of course, we will be totally distracted. Yet whatever we do outside cannot completely dissolve this silent suffering, the dis-satisfactoriness. Only embracing the interior life can quench it.

There are many forms of contemplation, but there is one very precious and important contemplation, and that is to reflect and realize how precious and how rare this human life is. We use many metaphors to bring about this understanding. One of them is remembering the *udumbara* flower. It is a mythological flower, a flower that is supposed to blossom once in many thousands of years. When it blossoms, it does not last for a long time. It decays easily. Now you see how rare, how precious this flower is. In the same way, this human life that you and I are enjoying is equally as (if not more) precious and rare as an *udumbara* flower. This understanding sounds so simple, but to feel it in your heart sometimes requires deep reflection, or sometimes a very powerful event in your life. It is important for us to take time to pause now and then and contemplate how amazing, how precious this human life is. Now and then when you are alone, when you are in nature, you feel this understanding. Your mind becomes so quiet. Your mind is no longer preoccupied by the past and the future. It is no longer busy with all your strategies, all your plans and projects. When your heart is completely open and quiet, you understand this truth naturally, the preciousness of your own human existence. Not only do you feel that your own life is precious, you feel that this whole existence is also precious and sacred. You feel that the clouds in the sky, the trees, the stones, everything is intrinsically sacred. Other times it requires a very shocking and even catastrophic event to bring about this understanding. It requires a crisis to motivate you to go inside and embrace this interior life.

I go to the southern part of the United States to cities like Austin, Texas, and Baton Rouge, Louisiana. There is a wonderful lady who comes to my retreat. She has been attending for almost three years. In the beginning, she always requested an interview, a meeting with me. She always looked unhappy and distraught. It turned out that she had an incurable disease. She wasn't able to have many things that other people have. The disease prevented her from achieving many desirable goals. Goals that everybody wants to realize. Perhaps she couldn't have a relationship either. This year she again came to my meditation retreat, and as usual she requested a meeting with me. To be honest, I had some kind of expectation, preconceived notions about my meeting with her. It turned out to be totally different. For the first time, she had a big smile on her face. She wasn't looking for clarity, guidance, or even answers from me. She wanted to share something with me. She wanted to share her inner transformation, a discovery of her interior life. She wanted to share a healing, a joy, a freedom with me. She told me that fundamentally she is happy. She is at peace. She also told me that she needed that disease. This is a very inspiring and courageous statement. She told me that if not for that incurable disease, she never would have found this spiritual path that she is walking. Her illness became a blessing in disguise. It became a powerful catalyst to show her the way to the interior life. And there she found love, courage, and compassion, which she might never have found without such a crisis.

Every now and then, we may need some kind of unsettling major crisis in our lives, such as illness, death and dying, or separation and loss, to wake our minds from this comfortable cradle of unconsciousness and turn our attention to our interior lives. Hopefully, none of us will have to go through an incurable disease to shake up our minds and turn our attention inward. All we need to do is start practicing contemplation. Through contemplation, we will soon realize that not only is this life precious, it is also very transient. It can come to an end at any given moment. Even if we live a hundred years, life is still very transient.

If we are in our forties or fifties, we are perhaps halfway through our lives. The first part of life is, in many senses, almost like a dream. It goes by in what seems like a single instant. When we try to look from hindsight, all we find sometimes is just this bundle of short memories, like snapshots. It is so much like a dream that we can describe the whole first half of our lives in a few words. We can describe it in a very ordinary fashion or in a very extravagant fashion. We can say, "I was born, I ate, I slept a lot, and now I'm here," or we can be a little more dramatic. We can polish this snapshot-like biography. We can say, "I was born with lots of rainbows. I became enlightened, and now I am here." We can, perhaps, write a whole book based on just what we did yesterday. At the same time, it feels like the first half of life is almost like a dream; it's already gone. When we look back, there are many things that make us truly happy. We may also have some regret or grief about our past. Every human being has his or her own regret, pain, and grief about the past. Sometimes we may wish we could go back, be born again, and start life all over—which is, of course, impossible. I am trying to point out that perhaps half of our lives is already gone with a mixture of grief, regret, joy, and rewarding moments.

Someday we will be lying on our deathbed. Hopefully, we will be surrounded by our loved ones. At that moment, our whole life will be gone in a single instant. This is why wise Buddhist masters are always encouraging us not to take this life for granted. They always say, "Don't waste this precious gift called your human life." What does it mean to not waste this precious life? Does it mean we should build a huge monument so people in the future remember us? Does it mean we should do something heroic and admirable? Does it mean we should climb Mount Everest, something that most people cannot do? When we hear the message to not waste this human life, we may feel that we *are* wasting our lives. We may feel we have to do something heroic, but the truth is that we don't. We don't have to try to climb to the top of Mount Everest. We don't have to build a grand monument. We don't have to compose a piece of music that people will play a hundred years from now. We can simply continue our lives as they are. Sometimes life can be very ordinary. We take our dog for a walk. We walk on the beach and pick up pebbles or build sand castles. It is so ordinary. Sometimes it is nice to be a child, isn't it? To be totally innocent? Sometimes it is liberating to be so ordinary.

In the end, there is no such thing as wasting your life. At the same time you realize the preciousness and the transient nature of life, you realize that this life is all about learning how to love. Everything that mattered so much in the past no longer matters. Isn't this extraordinary? It doesn't matter so much what you have and haven't achieved. All the things that mattered so much, things that imprisoned you in a world of hope and fear, no longer matter.

There is one thing that matters the most, and that is love. I am even a little bit reluctant to utter this word because it is too sacred. You know that in some traditions, like the Jewish tradition, there is this idea that they should not utter the name of the divine because it is too sacred. To me, this word *love* is like that.

Wouldn't it be funny to imagine that you were dying and were anxious about your hairstyle? Imagine that you are dying right now, within a few seconds, and are worrying about your weight. That would be very funny and a little bit insane. Imagine that you are dying, and you are asking people to carry you into the bathroom so you can look at yourself in the mirror because you are worried about your image. Wouldn't that be insane?

But the truth is that we *are* dying. The moment we are born, we are dying. We are, of course, living fully, but we are also dying. Every breath is actually the sound of the clock ticking. We are getting closer and closer to this world of the unknown, death. What will matter to us at that moment is love. I am not, of course, talking about ordinary love, romantic love. I'm speaking of true love, unconditional love, love that the mystics felt, love that the bodhisattvas felt. It is hard to define this love. It is about loving yourself and loving people around you and loving this world and loving life, loving the sorrow as well as the joy of this life. In the end, when you are dying, when you have just a few breaths left, there is one thing that will matter to you, and that is love. Then perhaps you will wish that you had loved more when you were alive.

It's not that I am asking you to love everybody right now. You won't perhaps be ready to love everyone on earth right now. This is going to be a journey, the journey of unconditional love, and you are going to meet lots of limitations. Your love will have limitations, which is totally acceptable. But there is going to be an evolution. As time goes by, your love will keep getting bigger and bigger. Your love will become more and more unconditional. You may be able to love somebody tomorrow whom you cannot love today. Or you may be able to love something that you can't love today.

CHAPTER TWELVE

# Your True Nature

THE NINETEENTH-CENTURY TIBETAN MASTER PATRUL
Rinpoche wrote many poems and dramas. One play, considered
one of the best literary works in the Tibetan language, opens with
a vivid image of a garden of lotuses. Some of them are tall, and some
are short. Some of them are blossoming, and some are decaying. He
used the variety of these lotuses to describe humanity. We are like
the variety of those lotuses. We are really different from each other.

When we look into the sky at night, there are countless stars
and planets. Each one is unique. When we walk on the beach, we
find countless grains of sand. Each grain of sand is totally different
from the others. We cannot find two grains of sand that are completely identical. In the forest, we find a variety of trees—redwoods,
eucalyptus, laurels, and so forth—each different from the others.
Somehow, in the world of nature, the uniqueness of everything is
expressed in harmony. The redwood never says, "I am better than the
eucalyptus. I am taller and bigger." The eucalyptus never says, "I'm

better because I have the best fragrance. My odor is more pleasant than that of any other tree." The trees don't compare themselves to each other to see which tree is the best. They don't have superiority and inferiority complexes. They exist in total harmony.

As human beings, we don't know how to accept and celebrate our own uniqueness while at the same time celebrating the uniqueness of others. We become very conscious of ourselves, whereas trees are not conscious of themselves. Being conscious of oneself is, of course, a big blessing. Through self-consciousness, we feel our own individuality. We have emotions and strengths with specific characteristics, flavors, and textures. We have our own dreams and visions and our own personal journey. We have our own desires. We can never fulfill our dreams by fulfilling the dreams of others. In the same way, we can never satisfy our own longings by satisfying the longings of other people. We have feelings that others cannot understand. We each have a life journey. Nobody knows how our life journey will unfold. Nobody has the absolute power to direct or influence our unfolding journey. So a lot of blessings come from being conscious of ourselves as individual human beings, unique entities in this giant universe.

At the same time, we have developed this habit of comparing ourselves to others. This constant habit of comparing ourselves to other people has turned out to be one of the most destructive human habits. It is the root of much of our misery, dissatisfaction, and even hatred. We cannot compare ourselves to anybody else. Everyone is unique, and everyone is perfect in their own uniqueness. Everyone is divine, sacred, and complete as they are. Nobody is better than anybody else. No one is less complete or less divine than anybody else.

We must realize that we are different from everybody else physically as well as mentally. There is only one version of you in this entire cosmos. There is no second you. You are truly rare and precious as you are. In the same way, everyone around you is totally rare and precious. You cannot find even one person in this world who is completely identical to you. Your body is unique and so are your psyche and your consciousness. Your personal stories are unique too. Everyone's biography is totally unique.

At the same time, we are all an expression of the truth that is indescribable. We are all the expression of buddha nature. Buddha nature is the basic ground of who we are. There is no division, no separation, no duality between you and me in the realm of the buddha nature. We are all an expression of it. Buddha nature manifests in each of us with a unique individuality of body, mind, and psyche. It is not something we can understand through intellect. Buddha nature—our true nature—is sacred, and our uniqueness, our bodies, our minds, are expressions of that sublime truth. Buddha nature is the most sacred thing that exists in this world. The most sacred thing is inside us. Our "beingness," our individuality, our uniqueness, are expressions of it. So what is most sacred does not lie outside; it lies within. This is why the Zen master Lin-Chi said, "If you run into Buddha on the street, kill him right there." He was saying that the true Buddha does not lie outside of you. I am not speaking about the historical Buddha, but the true Buddha, the *dharmakaya*, the infinite Buddha, is inside you. The very basic nature of your being is the highest Buddha. Everything about you—your hair, your nose, your skin, your mind, your qualities, even your flaws—is an expression of that which is most sacred.

When we compare ourselves to others, sometimes we may believe that we are better than they are. We may believe that we are smarter, more beautiful, more attractive, or more spiritual than other people. Then we feel conceited and prideful. Pride can be sometimes be quite pleasant; it can be a false bliss. This is why many people are trying to do everything in their power to maintain their pride, their sense of being better or more than others. Many people try to prove to the world that their achievements, their intellect, and their physical prowess show that somehow they are more than other people. On the other hand, sometimes we feel that there is someone out there who is more attractive, who has more money, or who is smarter than we are. Then we look at ourselves and feel incomplete and inferior, and we start criticizing and rejecting ourselves. This habit of comparing ourselves to others is deep-seated in us. We are not even conscious we are doing it most of the time, but we are always conducting our lives from this deep-seated tendency. This tendency is the very thing that is causing so much suffering in all of us.

The notion that there is some kind of fixed self with which we can identify is an illusion. The self that we identify as the one who is smart and beautiful, or not so smart and unattractive, is an illusion. Ultimately, we cannot identify ourselves with anything. Don't worry. I am not saying that you don't exist. You totally exist, but you are flowing energy. You are not a static entity that you can define, mold, categorize, or describe. You are indescribable. You are flowing energy: this living, vibrant collage of thoughts, emotions, conscious-ness, awareness, joy, and sadness. Therefore you are incomparable. You cannot compare yourself to anyone else because you are this flowing energy. You cannot hold on to any static version of your-self. You cannot say, "This is who I am, and I am going to compare myself to others." This fixed self is totally illusory. It only exists in your mind. It does not exist anywhere else.

Please don't think I am trying to be philosophical, not at all. I'm not opening some kind of complicated philosophical dialogue, arguing or analyzing whether the self exists or not. We can say that self does not exist, or we can say that self exists. Regardless, self is not static. Self is a living entity like a river, like a cloud. Sometimes when you look at a cloud, you can't hold on to anything because the cloud is changing constantly. Looking at the mist, you cannot hold on to it because it is always flowing. You cannot say this is beautiful mist or ugly mist or that this mist is good or bad. It is constantly flowing. The idea that there is some kind of fixed self that we can identify with and hold on to and compare with others is a total illusion. When you bring your attention toward yourself, you realize that you are very mysterious and multidimensional, a complex entity. You realize that you have many divine qualities like love, compassion, and awareness. You also find you have a lot of flaws, like everyone else. You have your own imperfections. You have your weaknesses. At the same time, you realize sooner or later that the ground of your being is already perfect as it is. The ground of your being is nonconceptual. You cannot understand it by analyzing it.

Just a few weeks ago, a Zen monk came to my meditation retreat. He must be in his sixties. He is a monk, a very sincere and open-hearted person. He asked me to have a little time with him. He wanted to share his spiritual journey with me. Also he wanted my opinion on whether he had had a satori experience or not. Satori is a very big thing in Zen Buddhism; *satori* means "sudden enlightenment." He told me that when he entered the monastery, his master gave him a koan, just one question. He didn't speak any English. The translator said the koan, or question, was this: "What brings about this life?" The monk kept pondering and meditating on that one question every day for a long time. He meditated in the temple from morning to evening every day. Finally he felt that he was able to answer that koan, yet his master didn't accept his answer. Unfortunately, the master passed away before the monk could get an affirmation from him. At some point at the meditation retreat, we were dancing, and he got up and started dancing in front of everybody. He was dancing in his gray robes. Perhaps he had never danced in his life, and this was the first time. We were doing a Tibetan Buddhist ceremony, a sacred feast where we eat, dance, and sing. He was dancing beautifully. I felt that he didn't have anything to learn from me. He came there just to dance. I felt that he came to my meditation retreat to learn how to dance. He knew everything already, except how to dance. I felt that his dancing was the answer to his koan.

A koan doesn't seek a conceptual answer. There are things we can't understand through intellect, such as a koan. One of the koans in the Zen Buddhist tradition is, "What is your face before you were born?" This koan is not stating that there is actually some kind of concrete or physical face before you were born. It is a metaphorical question. This koan is pointing out that there is true nature in each of us, the *dharmakaya,* the highest Buddha, which is totally non-conceptual. In the realm of our true nature, we are perfect. We are beautiful, rich, and complete. We lack nothing.

Once you are able to let go of your attachment to all these fixed notions of yourself, all your fixed identities, then you are free inside. Finally you can fall in love with yourself. That is the end of comparing yourself to others. Then you will know that your true nature is complete and perfect, the most sacred thing, and then you can celebrate your uniqueness. This is very much the wisdom of Tantric Buddhism, which teaches that the highest *sadhana* is to worship yourself, to worship your body, to worship your mind. When you eat food, eat everything with this sacred outlook. Think that you are the deity. Your body is the divine abode. You know, in the East, people worship deities such as Avalokiteshvara, Guanyin, and Tara. There are many temples enshrining the images of those divinities. People go to the temples, sing songs, and offer flowers and food to worship the deities. Tantric Buddhism teaches that the highest *sadhana,* the highest teaching, is to worship yourself completely. When you eat food, don't eat with an ordinary outlook. Think that you are making an offering, a sacred offering to a deity. Your food is the sacred offering, and you are the deity. Your body is the mandala, the divine abode.

Tantric Buddhism teaches that the highest *sadhana* is to love your body, to love your mind, to love your glory, and to love your imperfections. Hold all your imperfections and your glories as unique expressions of the highest Buddha, the *tathagatagarbha,* the *dharmakaya.* Your job is to recognize that we are all an expression of *tathagatagarbha* and to celebrate your uniqueness. Your job is to notice, recognize, and celebrate everything about yourself. Celebrate your problems, your shortcomings, your weaknesses, as well as your intelligence, strength, and holiness.

# CHAPTER THIRTEEN

# Leave Your Mind Alone

Usually we are busy taking care of our daily affairs. We are very good at maintaining our conventional business. We go to see a doctor periodically to make sure we are healthy. We often spend a lot of resources remodeling or renovating our homes. We hire people to fix the garden and take care of the lawn. Now and then we also check our bank account to make sure there is enough money. As human beings, we are very good at taking care of the exterior world. Somehow we are almost lost in the outer world. At the same time, the mind has been neglected. We don't spend enough time taking care of our own minds. From that point of view, to be spiritual is quite simple. It means someone spends lots of time taking care of his or her own mind. It is not about being holy. It is not about being different from ordinary people in conventional society. It simply means that you spend some time looking after your mind in the same way that you look after your house, your hair, your health, and your bank account.

The consequences of neglecting the mind can be quite serious. Perhaps most of our pain and misery come from simply neglecting our own minds. Sooner or later we will come to the shocking conclusion that a huge percentage of our suffering is unnecessary. In some ways, this is good news. We may realize that a huge percentage of our suffering is not derived from something being intrinsically wrong with us. It is not from a lack of food, sickness, or physical separation from our loved ones. Instead, it comes from simply neglecting our minds. So being spiritual is very simple. It is not about being religious or being a saint. It is not about being holier than other people. It is all about spending some time taking care of the mind. This human mind is very powerful. It can be benevolent, and it can also be malevolent. It can be quite destructive.

First, we must be very thankful to have our human minds. Imagine that you had a human body without a human mind. You would be very funny. You wouldn't even be like a human being without this mind. The mind is the most important element in what makes us human beings. We are a unique species in this world. We can think. We can be self-conscious. We can make the connection between the past and the future and between cause and effect. We can hate ourselves. We can love ourselves. Many species are not able to do these things. So this human mind is a very powerful force. It is as powerful as a tornado, a volcano, or an earthquake. It is so powerful that it can be destructive when it is neglected. It can also be beautiful and benevolent, especially when we look after it.

The ancient meditators discovered that the human mind is usually troubled, unruly, destructive, and uncontrollable. They came up with the expression "monkey mind" to describe it. We all have monkey mind. Sometimes we are not aware that we have this monkey mind. When we meditate, the best and even most inspiring insight is not about waking up and having a transcendent epiphany. It is not about feeling enlightened or feeling that we have awakened to our true nature as an inborn buddha. It is also not about having mind-tripping sacred visions. Instead, the most inspiring insight we can have is discovering that we have monkey mind. When I lead a meditation retreat, and people tell me that they feel they are enlightened, I may want to run away because I feel the whole situation is hopeless. I can't help them. They have nothing to learn from me. But when people say they discovered that they have monkey mind, I am happy and thrilled. I feel that I can help them, that they have something to learn from me.

So don't worry about discovering buddha mind in yourself. Let go of your obsession with buddha-mind, cosmic consciousness, and so forth. Instead, let's go inside and find this thing called monkey mind. We know that there is monkey mind in all of us. Often we are unaware of our own minds; the monkey mind has been ruling us. We have been literally controlled and enslaved by this monkey mind, which is unconscious of itself. True reflection, true meditation, is really about looking inside and paying attention to the mind. It is also about taking care of the mind and about honestly observing what is happening in that interior world. We may end up realizing through such reflection that we have been lost in the exterior world. We have been busy trying to run away from unfavorable circumstances and chasing after favorable ones. We don't realize that both happiness and suffering are mainly just two different states of our own minds. We don't realize that we can never arrive at true fulfillment and joy unless we begin to pay attention to our own minds.

When we pay attention to the mind, we see that there are lots of old mental habits. We also see that these mental habits, thoughts, and emotions are completely ruling us. They are unconsciously motivating us to engage in actions that are sometimes quite destructive, actions that can be aggressive, harmful, and even violent. Basically we begin to be aware that there is a lot of messiness, or even mental garbage, in each of us. When we discover that, it is a true sign that our spiritual path is going well. It is an indication that we are walking the right path, that we are going in the right direction. It is also a sign that we know how to meditate. The mind can be like a house that is falling apart, like a meadow covered with poisonous trees and plants. This is what we see when we truly look inside. This is how the ancient meditators found the monkey mind in themselves.

When we meditate, we do not look for divine signs of enlightenment. Instead, we look for this monkey mind, this mental garbage. The more we meditate, the more we become aware of this mental garbage that we all have. This mental garbage is filled with old emotions, destructive thoughts, greed, fear, hatred, and so forth. Once we become aware of it, there may be a natural impulse to transcend it. It is a very inspiring as well as enticing desire. Believe it or not, I have spent a big part of my life attempting to transcend my own mind. In the end, I came to the understanding that we cannot transcend the mind; we can't make it go away. We cannot transcend our thoughts, and we cannot transcend our fears. What is required is the deep inquiry. The deep inquiry here is looking into our own minds, into the depths of our own thoughts and emotions. Through such deep inquiry, we discover that there is not much solidity or truth there. We find out that there is no truth, no validity, no concreteness, in our thoughts and feelings or even in our consciousness. This is why Buddha said that feelings, are like a bubble and perceptions are like a mirage. The bubbles in water look so real, but if we touch them, there is no essence in them. A mirage looks real, but if we try to walk into it or grasp it, we find that there is nothing there. In the same way, we do not find any substance when we look into our thoughts and minds. The foundation of our thoughts, emotions, and minds is completely unreal, insubstantial, empty. Because of this lack of reality and substance, we can let go of these mental constructs right now or hold on to them as long as we want. We can hold on to our thoughts for decades and decades or even for the rest of our lives. Of course, we suffer from holding on to our attachment to thoughts and emotions. It can also lead us into harmful and even destructive actions. We can believe in the mind and our thoughts as long as we want, or we can stop believing them right now and simply let go of them. We have this choice. Isn't this an amazing choice? Self-loathing is a thought. We can believe it forever and suffer inside, or we can stop believing it. Then we are free in that very moment.

Of course, there are many thought patterns happening in our minds every day. Perhaps there are one or two or three thought patterns that we don't know how to go beyond. They are like invisible entities, demons chasing us and haunting us. We feel that we cannot be happy, we cannot be in harmony with our lives, as long as we are haunted by these thought patterns in our minds. A thought pattern can be anger. It can be insecurity. It can be fear. It can be a belief system. Next time one of these thought patterns arises, take a moment to look deeply into it until you find that its foundation is insubstantial, illusory, empty. Once you discover that the patterns are empty in themselves, don't pay attention to them. Just leave them alone. Don't pick them up, and sooner or later they may just go away.

As long as we keep on believing that the mind is real or concrete, we will not know how to do this very simple work, which is to leave the mind alone. Leave thoughts alone. Don't follow or pick up your thoughts. This understanding can come into being through inquiry. The traditional inquiry is to go inside and look for the source of your mind. You can even keep asking, "Where does this mind come from? Where does it dissolve?" Sometimes all we need is a few minutes of this inquiry, and then we realize the foundation of the mind is empty. Sometimes we may have to spend more than a few minutes. We may need days or months to come to this profound understanding. With this understanding, we will know how to apply this very simple method of leaving the mind alone. Actually, it's not a method; it's a methodless method. It's just leaving your mind and your thoughts alone. It's not believing, chasing, and following the thoughts in your mind. It sounds so ordinary and simplistic. It sounds ordinary and simplistic to the spiritual ego because nothing is happening when we stop believing the mind. Many great masters of the past said there is nothing to be found in the end. This is why a famous Tibetan master said that not finding is the great finding. When you stop believing your mind, there is nothing to be found.

You aren't finding anything. You've simply stopped believing your own mind. You are not finding enlightenment, you are not finding nirvana, and you are not finding eternity. Yet there is so much spaciousness, freedom. There is openness when you stop believing your own mind. That openness is some kind of inexhaustible source from which love and peace can arise.

Let's make today a day of peace. Let's dedicate this day as a day to stop believing our minds. True inner peace can only arise when you stop believing your own mind. As long as you believe your own mind, there is no peace, either inside or outside. Let's stop believing our thoughts, our emotions, and our perceptions for a while.

# CHAPTER FOURTEEN

# Timeless Sacredness

Wहen people have an existential crisis or when they do deep reflection, they begin to ask questions that normal people don't ask, such as, "Why am I here? Why is there a universe in the first place? Why does everything exist?" Most of the time, we don't understand why we are here or why we came into being in the first place or why all of the events that have occurred in our lives since we were born have happened. Many events and circumstances take place in life. Some of them are challenging, and some of them are exciting and rewarding, a source of joy. And we cannot always forecast the future. We have no control over our future. The future is always the greatest unknown. We cannot predict what is going to happen tomorrow. We don't know what is going to happen to each of us tomorrow or even this evening. So there is always this unknown and great mystery that seems to be the foundation of our existence. The very foundation of our existence is not something we can predict or comprehend. Instead, it always remains unknown, the greatest unknown. Many events have happened to each of us that we still don't understand. We get sick periodically, and we get rewarded now and then. We are born at a certain time and place. We don't understand why all these things happened, and we don't understand what is going to happen in the future.

Of course, sometimes we can use our thinking mind to analyze and try to figure out why something happened, why we are here, and what is going to happen tomorrow. We can understand the causes and conditions to a certain extent, yet there is always the great mystery. This great mystery is not to be solved. We can call this unknown, this great mystery, karma. We can say everything is our own karma. Yet we can never understand karma. That's why many of the ancient Eastern philosophers said, "Don't analyze karma because we can never fully understand it." The idea of karma is that we will never completely understand the mystery of our existence. Sometimes we hope there is a clear explanation for everything and there will be a remedy, a solution for all our problems, especially the problems we don't like. We have small problems and big problems. Small problems are those like losing our hair. Lots of people are working with that, trying to come up with a remedy. Then we have a big problem, which is our mortality. Of course, our desire is to live a long life or maybe even live forever. Living forever is completely impossible, and still many people have this desire now and then. The point is that we are here, and there is nothing we can do about it. It is too late to change our minds. Welcome to this planet. We are completely here, and so far there isn't any exit strategy. So we might as well enjoy this world to the best of our ability.

It seems like there is some kind of cosmic desire that wants to exist. Not desire as an instinctual desire, but desire as a force, an almost eternal force. As the ancient wise men and women said, the universe has no beginning and no end. This is an amazing theory that the universe has no beginning and no end and that there is an eternal force, this eternal desire that wants to exist. Out of that eternal desire, everything comes into being—everything from the smallest to the most infinite reality, including the speck of dust on a cushion. Throughout the universe, they all come into being through this eternal desire. The eternal desire in itself is sacred. It is not impure. It is not simple. We all come into being through that force. So from that point of view, we are born out of sacredness. Not out of original sin but out of original sacredness.

There is nothing wrong with having the desire to exist. When we look around, we see that everything has this desire to exist. Trees, flowers, mountains all have it. We can see that desire to exist in ourselves. Sometimes it is very rational, and sometimes it is very irrational. When we are sick, we want to live a long time. Not for selfish reasons. We want to live to be around our loved ones. We want to help them, and such a desire is rational and heroic. Sometimes our desire to live and to exist is just pure instinct. There is no logic behind it. In the end, we just have to leave everything up to this great mystery we should call karma. It's all karma. Why I am here, everything that has happened in my life, and everything that is going to happen to me is my own karma. The good news is that you are never going to understand karma. That is good news, isn't it? Remember, the great ancient masters said, "Don't analyze your karma." You don't have to figure everything out. You can leave everything up to the great mystery, the great unknown.

Buddha said that the root of all human suffering is craving. He talked about three types of craving: craving for existence, craving for sensual pleasure, and craving for nonexistence. This way of shedding light on the very root of human suffering is the least abstract and least conceptual. It is very scientific and psychological. Sometimes they say that the root of human suffering is ignorance, which is hard to understand because the idea of ignorance, primordial ignorance, sometimes sounds very abstract. But craving is not abstract. It's something we can truly relate to. Everybody can relate to the idea of craving. We can really understand this notion with our minds, our bodies, and our bones. The Buddha said that all human suffering comes into being through these three cravings.

The first one is craving for existence. Craving is more than just instinctual desire. Remember that all of our instincts, all of our desires, are fine in themselves. You know how sometimes we have to put everything into categories? Can there be something that is neither sacred nor profane, neither pure nor impure, neither good nor bad? If you really love to put things in categories, then I recommend that you put your desire, your instinct, even your eternal desire to exist, into the category of "sacred." Or you don't have to call it sacred. Just leave it alone.

The universe's desire to exist is just fine in itself. Embrace it; honor it without having any guilt about it. The desire is natural. But craving is something different. Craving is sometimes unnatural. Your desire to exist is natural. It is uncontrived. What is natural is usually healthy. You know there is a healthy state of mind, and then there is an unhealthy state of mind. There is a healthy instinct and an unhealthy instinct. Your desire to exist is totally healthy because it is natural. You are born with it. Craving seems to be unhealthy. It is more like a neurotic level of desire. It's almost like a neurotic obsession to exist, and that craving is usually accompanied by lots of fear and insecurity. It is a fear of death, and it sometimes comes with violence. There is violence in fighting against reality, impermanence, and change. Perhaps you have heard that many Zen masters claim they have transcended life and death. Can you really transcend death? It depends on how we understand what it means to transcend death. From one perspective, we cannot transcend death; we are all going to die. On the other hand, we can transcend death. At the moment we are able to cut through and let go of our craving for existence, we have transcended death. Then there is no more fear of death. Then there is total acceptance.

Many years ago, I was visiting this beautiful Buddhist monastery in Indiana. They invited me to lead a meditation retreat. Then I got a message all the way from Tibet that my grandmother was dying. We used social media to communicate with my friends and especially with my grandmother, who raised me. She was like my mother in many ways. At that point, she couldn't talk; she was almost gone. As a tradition, I offered prayers to her and for her and for everyone around her. Somehow I felt this peace, just an unbelievable level of peace, by watching her face and being in her presence. She was almost gone, she couldn't talk, and perhaps she couldn't really see my face at all, but there was so much peace. There was no grief inside me. I don't know whether this is good or not. There was no more grief, no more sadness, no more struggle. There was total acceptance inside me. Somehow this voice kept coming from my heart. It was not me that was talking. The voice said to her, "It's time for you to go. This is the best time for you to go. You have had enough of everything. You have lived your life fully. Now don't live anymore. This is the perfect day that you can go away." When I looked at her presence, I saw that there was no fear, and there was not even the slightest sense of resistance. So it's very strange that I didn't have any grief after she was gone. Of course, we all want to live, but at the same time we always have to be ready to accept our own impermanence, our own mortality. In some traditions, they teach you at a very early age how to contemplate your own mortality, your own fragile reality.

Out of craving, this kind of neurotic obsession with our own existence, many other forms of craving come into being. Craving for security, success, power, affection, recognition, certainty, wealth, and so forth. Craving for comfort, craving for favorable circumstances. And we see that clearly much of our suffering comes into being from these cravings. Actually if you look into consciousness right now, maybe you will find suffering. Do you find suffering? Maybe you are not suffering right now, but is there suffering inside you? This is a powerful inquiry. This is the most powerful form of self-inquiry, the most powerful form of self-reflection. It is easy to do this inquiry. We don't have to go into the mountains or into the forest to do this reflection.

So I am asking you to look inside and find out whether there is pain inside you, whether there is suffering. Of course, suffering is a universal situation. We all have suffering. So acknowledge it here. Feel it. Embrace it. Hold it. Don't try to reject it. We cannot reject suffering. We cannot remove it. We cannot transcend it. This is why Buddha said, "One must inquire in order to understand the root of suffering." He never said transcend suffering. He said realize suffering and cut through to the root of it. This is such a wise statement. Have you ever had this beautiful delusion, after you started on this spiritual journey, that somehow there is a way you can transcend suffering? Some people have this delusion. Some people, when they walk the spiritual path, they go through this stage where they may believe they can transcend their suffering, go beyond all this earthly reality, and live in the heavenly reality forever. But Buddha said, "Just realize your suffering." He didn't say transcend it or remove it or get rid of it.

I am asking you to realize your own suffering. Realize your own suffering through your body, through your bones, through your marrow. Not through your intellect. Feel your suffering now and then. And if you keep feeling your own suffering without any resistance, with love and with courage, then sooner or later there is a natural inquiry that happens. Which will lead you to the understanding that all your suffering (or most of it) comes from craving, craving for something. The object of craving changes, believe it or not, because it is not rational in the first place. We are craving this and that, craving comfort and recognition, craving personal glory, and craving for some ideal circumstance. We want it so much, and we think that until we have it, life is empty and incomplete. Recognize the object of your craving. This craving is not natural to us. Desire is natural to us, but craving is neurotic. Craving is a form of desire that becomes neurotic. Desire that has lost its original quality, its natural quality.

Recognize your suffering as well as its root and then learn to let go of it. Sometimes you will find a place inside yourself where there is no more craving, where it is already free. This is why we meditate. When our minds and bodies are completely serene, we feel that we are standing on the ground somewhere inside ourselves where there is no more craving and no more fear. This is the natural state of our being. The natural state of our being is already free from craving. If you are religious, then you can offer all your craving to the divine. In India, you can offer everything to Kali, the goddess of destruction. If you are a Buddhist, you can offer all your craving to the great emptiness. If you are none of these, then you can offer all your craving to the great mystery, the huge vacuum cleaner called the cosmos. It sucks all of your craving away from you if you offer it.

It is beautiful that we exist. Have you ever had a moment when you were simply enjoying that you exist? A moment when you were so serene, and you simply enjoyed being alive? You enjoyed that you were breathing, that you could smell, that you could feel and taste? In moments like this, we feel so much joy. We enjoy the fact that we are simply alive in that very moment, that we exist right now.

# CHAPTER FIFTEEN

# Your Heart Wants to Dance

SHANTIDEVA WROTE MANY POEMS AND PRAYERS. EVEN though they were written hundreds of years ago, people are still studying his writings and reciting his prayers. In one of his poems, he writes, "May we hear the sound of dharma from birds, trees, plants, and the sky." This is quite a powerful prayer. Maybe it is metaphorical, but hearing the sound of dharma from all these inanimate objects is an interesting idea, and in many ways it makes sense. The sound of dharma is the spiritual teachings of the Buddha. Perhaps we won't literally be able to hear the sound of dharma or the Buddha's teachings from things like birds, trees, and plants. But we can hear the Buddha's teachings from many sources, especially from people, from the lives of individuals. We find many inspiring stories in the lives of courageous human beings.

Recently I was having lunch with someone who said he knew a man who is enlightened. The man lost his eyesight from a disease—multiple sclerosis—and my friend told me that this man is enlightened. It is inspiring to hear that there are amazing human beings on this planet who are courageous and maybe even enlightened. My friend told me that the man has a secret, a spiritual secret: the secret to freedom and of absolute happiness. Intellectually, his secret is challenging, but it is quite simple. His secret to enlightenment is "just surrender." It turns out that all he practices is constant surrender. Surrendering to everything—surrendering to life, surrendering to suffering, and surrendering to difficult circumstances like losing his sight.

It must be very challenging, almost unthinkable, to lose your sight and then live in joy without closing your heart. The moment we close our hearts, we cannot feel in harmony with everything around us. Then we don't know how to love; we don't know how to care for somebody else; we don't know how to have compassion. We become bitter inside. We become like a Grinch inside. Perhaps many of you know the Grinch. He is a very powerful archetype of someone with a closed heart who is totally bitter. So the story my friend told me was the sound of dharma. When we go around with open eyes and ears, many spiritual teachings coming from every source, every direction. This story was the sound of dharma for me. I didn't have to read an ancient scripture or go to a formal sermon. I just heard it as something spontaneous in an ordinary conversation. When we hear inspiring stories like this, something wakes up inside our consciousness. We feel that we understand something we haven't understood in the past. We want to say, "This is it! This is the heart of the matter." Synchronistically, the day before I heard this story I gave a talk on surrender. I feel that the very heart of Buddhist teachings is surrender. The heart of Buddhism is simple as well as singular. There is not much to talk about. It is all about surrender.

Surrendering is the shortcut to freedom. If anybody wants a shortcut to freedom, then surrender is it. Everybody loves the idea of a shortcut. They want a shortcut to enlightenment, a shortcut to freedom, and there have been many rumors about such shortcuts. Some say there is a shortcut to enlightenment. We'll see about that. Have you ever run into anybody who found it and became enlightened? Have you ever met anyone who was truly enlightened because he or she discovered the shortcut? If there is such a thing as the direct, most dynamic way to freedom and unconditional happiness, then it must be the act of surrender. This is the only possibility. Sometimes surrender is so simple, yet we aren't willing to do it. It is said that sometimes we are forced to surrender when there is great suffering in our lives. When we are dying, when a tragedy strikes us or our loved ones, or when we lose everything, then we have no choice except to surrender. In an amazing way, suffering can force us to become free, awake, and liberated inside.

In the old days, the skillful masters sometimes accepted a few disciples and taught them how to surrender. It can be a very long process, just like the story about Naropa and Tilopa or the story about Marpa and Milarepa. What happened between these students and masters was very unconventional and a bit too radical for today. You may have read about the Tibetan yogi Milarepa who is considered the most amazing spiritual teacher, a *mahasiddha* in Tibetan Buddhist tradition. When Milarepa met with his master, Marpa, Marpa told him to build five castles. His master didn't give him any good reason why he was to build the castles. Not only that, every time Milarepa finished building a castle, Marpa demanded that he dismantle it and put every rock back where it came from. What is amazing about this story is that Marpa was so selfless that he didn't have any selfish motive with his disciple, Milarepa. He gave these radical disciplines and practices out of total love, egoless love. Otherwise it would have been a form of abuse and exploitation. It is said that Marpa didn't teach Milarepa anything for a long time. Even though Milarepa went to Marpa to study Buddhism, Marpa didn't teach him any Buddhism for a long time. Instead he gave him this unconventional assignment. It turned out that Marpa was teaching Milarepa how to surrender.

It sounds like there are two ways we can learn how to surrender: through an unbelievable level of tragedy and suffering, or through studying with an extraordinary master like Marpa and having the willingness to undertake an unconventional process. Perhaps there are other ways to learn how to surrender. Maybe we don't have to suffer as much. We definitely don't have to find this kind of radical master to learn how to surrender. Surrender is a state of mind. Something we can do even in this very moment. Perhaps many of us have had moments of surrender here and there. We know how liberating and freeing it is when we know how to truly surrender. When we completely surrender to life, we surrender to happiness, suffering, birth, death, failure, and tragedy as well as to glory, joy, and thousands of blessings. We let go of all our attachments and obsessions. We let go of the powerful fantasies that torture us and don't allow us to be blissful inside, that don't allow our hearts to dance.

Believe it or not our hearts are wild dancers, ecstatic dancers. They always want to dance. We may remember when we were children; our hearts were always dancing. Our hearts didn't know how to hate, how to be greedy or selfish, how to have resentment, or how to be judgmental. Our hearts were innocent. We played with toys—sticks, rocks, and trees. When we remember this, we see that the heart is a natural, blissful dancer. It always wants to dance. It wants to be in harmony with everything. It wants to surrender. It wants to love. It wants to melt. It wants to forgive. It wants to be spacious. It wants to transcend all the limitations, all the boundaries. The heart wants to be graceful like the sea and spacious like the sky.

Somehow our hearts are not dancing. Of course, there are many moments when we are in touch with that pure, original, innocent heart. In those moments, we become naturally generous, courageous, and loving. In the moments when your heart is not dancing, a good thing to do is to go inside and simply ask, "Is my heart dancing? Is my heart dancing in unconditional love, in joy, and in peace?" This is a very powerful inquiry even though the wording sounds so simple. Your heart knows how to dance and sing songs. It knows how to love in the midst of tragedy and sorrow. Your heart knows how to love the enemy who causes you so much pain.

*Bodhicitta* is the most beautiful state of mind we can experience. Some people translate *bodhicitta* as the "enlightened mind," which is a wonderful translation but a little too grand. Others translate *bodhicitta* as the "awakened heart," which is a beautiful translation. Mahayana Buddhism says that *bodhicitta* is this amazing mind that you can have before you become a buddha, before you become fully enlightened. It teaches that you can develop *bodhicitta,* the awakened heart, right now, no matter who you are. It says you can develop *bodhicitta* even when you are lost in a delusion, in a totally painful state of mind. This is quite an inspiring message. We don't have to become enlightened, and we don't have to be buddhas to give rise to *bodhicitta.* We can give rise to *bodhicitta,* the awakened heart, right now. In some ways, our hearts are awakened on their own; our hearts are already awakened. This is now a time to surrender, to let our hearts dance. Remember that the only way your heart can dance is through your readiness to surrender. Surrender to everything and let go of all your hopes, all your fears. Let go of all your attachment, your hatred. Try to do that for even a single moment and see what happens.

The thirteenth-century Zen master Bunan wrote this beautiful poem: "Die while you are alive and be absolutely dead, and then you can do whatever you want, it's all good." This is quite a thought-provoking poem. It can take many years of Buddhist practice to understand it because it is so subtle, so simple and yet so subtle. The poem is not intellectually potent. In fact, it doesn't make sense intellectually. There is no knowledge, no information, and no theory in this poem. It is very simple. This is why when you begin to arrive—not on the surface, but at the heart of the Buddhism—it becomes less and less conceptual. It becomes more and more simple, more and more experiential, more and more poetic. It becomes subtler and subtler.

Have you ever entertained your mind by thinking about what it would be like to die? I used to entertain this thought when I was very young. What would happen when I died? There was a fear, but then I thought I would be this spirit. I used to meditate on this, which is very interesting. I would become this spirit. I could fly everywhere, travel everywhere. I had no more wants. I wouldn't need anything. I would no longer care how I looked. I would not care what happened to me because I was dead. But when I was thinking about death, I did not think of it like some kind of nihilistic state, like the end of everything. I thought of it more like a state in which I would become a spirit, a flying spirit. The truth is that we can be flying spirits right now. We can fly into the space called human life, and we don't have to worry or even care about who we are or what we have or don't have. We don't have to care about whether we have a lot of money or not or whether we have a relationship or not. Maybe we do not have to care about whether we are sick or not. Maybe we don't even care if we have eyes or not, just like that amazing person we heard about earlier.

Surrendering and letting go of all our attachments and all our obsessions is a form of dying. It is a death for our ego at least. Many masters in the past actually went through this process. They totally died inside. They lived as these flying spirits. Of course we can't literally die while we are alive. We know that. As a reflection, don't you think it would be really amazing and freeing if we could really die while we were alive? If we could do that literally, which is impossible, then we would lose all our fears, all our hopes, all our greed, all our ambitions. When we lose all of that, the only thing we can experience is love, and we will be able to love everyone. Then we will be able to live in the present moment, and our hearts will dance eternally.

In some sense, maybe there is a way we can die while we are alive. Remember, it is part of surrendering. It is to let go of all our obsessions, all our greed, all our fear, and all our hatred. Can we do that in this very moment? Usually there is a powerful resistance to that. Try to see where the resistance comes from. We realize that the resistance does not come from the heart. It does not come from the depth of our being. It comes from the ego, from the human ego. What would happen if we let go of everything? If we really let go of everything, all our fears, all our hopes, we wouldn't end up on the street, even though our ego may tell us that. It may give us these false warning signs.

What would happen if we really let go of everything, everything that binds us, everything that makes us suffer? The only thing that is going to happen is that our hearts will dance again, and we will feel so much freedom, so much joy, that we cannot hold it inside.

Actually, we don't have to try to surrender. That sounds too effortful. Then we will have a surrender competition. There is going to be a spiritual marathon, a spiritual Olympics, how about that? Indeed, there is a spiritual Olympics. It is not officially announced. Many people are working really hard trying to be the best meditator, the best ascetic, the most enlightened. So don't try to surrender with your personal will or deliberate effort. It sounds like too much work, trying to surrender to everything. Instead, go inside. That is all you need to do sometimes. Go inside and let yourself be in touch with your heart. You know how to be in touch with your heart. Your heart is waiting to be recognized. This is why the Tibetan masters often said there are many forms or levels of meditation. The highest level is what they call effortless meditation. When they teach how to meditate, especially the masters from the Nyingma tradition, they always say, "Don't do anything." Rest in the present moment. Relax in the natural state of your mind, because if you can relax, rest in the natural state of your own mind, then you will be in touch with your own heart, with your original heart, with your innocent heart, and then surrender is very easy because all of your heart wants it.

Dharmata
FOUNDATION

ANAM THUBTEN travels nationally and internationally to teach and conduct meditation retreats. To view Anam Thubten's teaching and retreat schedule, please visit:

https://www.dharmata.org/events-calendar/

Other inquiries may be directed to:

info@dharmata.org

or

Dharmata Foundation
235 Washington Avenue
Point Richmond, CA 94801
510-233-7071
Website: https://www.dharmata.org/